ANTIFASCISM, SPORTS, SOBRIETY
Forging a Militant Working-Class Culture
Selected Writings by Julius Deutsch

Edited and Translated by Gabriel Kuhn

Antifascism, Sports, Sobriety: Forging a Militant Working-Class Culture
Edited and translated by Gabriel Kuhn
© 2017 PM Press.

ISBN: 978-1-62963-154-7
Library of Congress Control Number: 20169930974

Cover photograph courtesy of Arbeitsgemeinschaft für Sport
und Körperkultur in Österreich (ASKÖ) / Confédération Sportive
Internationale Travailliste et Amateur (CSIT)
Cover by John Yates / www.stealworks.com
Interior design by briandesign

10 9 8 7 6 5 4 3 2 1

PM Press
PO Box 23912
Oakland, CA 94623
www.pmpress.org

Printed in the USA by the Employee Owners of Thomson-Shore in
Dexter, Michigan.
www.thomsonshore.com

Contents

About This Book

Historical works always have documentary value. In this case, people interested in the history of European socialism, Austromarxism, the interwar period, the workers' movement, and specifically workers' militias, workers' sport, and workers' sobriety will come across relevant material and find texts available in English for the first time. Usually, however, this alone does not explain the motivation for putting a historical work together. Often, there is the hope attached that revisiting historical debates can inform current ones. In this case, two aspects seem to be of particular relevance:

1. It seems important to reconceptualize the historical workers' movement as a *cultural* movement. The historical workers' movement was not reduced to economic and political struggles, or, to be more precise, it considered it impossible to separate cultural struggles from economic and political ones. While contemporary forms of crude workerism tend to reduce working-class politics to labor-related issues, the early twentieth-century workers' movement aimed at no less than creating new human beings who, in turn, would create a new society. The historical workers' movement addressed all aspects of everyday existence, including some—such as sports and drink—that might be considered bourgeois, middle class, or lifestylist by contemporary activists. Never was this more obvious than in the Red Vienna

of the 1920s, governed by the Austromarxist leaders
of Austria's *Sozialdemokratische Arbeiterpartei* (Social
Democratic Workers' Party, SDAP).

2. It seems important to rekindle debates about
    Austromarxism, a unique chapter in socialism's history.
    The Austromarxist school was characterized by a dedi-
    cated attempt to unite the workers' movement across
    ideological lines. There is little English material avail-
    able on its history, and even in the German-speaking
    world it has often been ignored. But at a time when
    the Left is on the defensive and the combined threat
    of neoliberalism and neofascism seems to make left-
    wing unity mandatory, it is crucial to learn from past
    attempts at forming broad working-class alliances, and
    to examine both their achievements and their failures.

The book is divided into two parts: an introductory essay
about Red Vienna, its working-class culture, and its eventual
defeat; and a selection of writings by Julius Deutsch.

While Julius Deutsch has never been one of
Austromarxism's leading theorists, he was one of the tendency's key organizers and represented its approach and
its understanding of working-class struggle like few others.
This is particularly true for its physical—or "muscular"—part,
which in German is fittingly called *Körperkultur*, literally, "body
culture." Deutsch was the chairman of the *Republikanische
Schutzbund* (Republican Defense League), an organization
of antifascist workers' militias; the president of the Socialist
Workers' Sport International; and an important personality in
the Austrian *Arbeiter-Abstinentenbund* (Workers' Temperance
League). The combination is far from random. Militancy,
sports, and sobriety went hand in hand in Red Vienna when
it came to celebrating the culture of the body.

The book focuses on the physical aspects of workers'
culture because they have been the most neglected in

historical accounts. There exist far more studies about workers' education, literature, theater, and other intellectual and artistic pursuits than the physicality of the proletarian movement. The latter, however, was at the heart of the Austromarxist experience, not least because the ever-growing fascist threat it faced demanded physical defense. It was no coincidence that after the defeat of the socialist workers' militias in the Austrian Civil War of 1934, the leading Austromarxist theorist Otto Bauer singled out the workers' sport and temperance organizations in describing the dire consequences:

"All workers' associations have been dissolved: the sports clubs of the working youth; the big Alpine hiking association the Friends of Nature, which has led tens of thousands of workers from inns to noble pleasures; the Workers' Temperance League, which has saved thousands of proletarians from the dangers of alcoholism and thereby the dignity and happiness of thousands of families—all of the precious work, indeed all of it, that the workers' movement has done for mass culture has been destroyed."[1]

Gabriel Kuhn, October 2014

Notes

1   Otto Bauer, *Der Aufstand der österreichischen Arbeiter. Seine Ursachen und seine Wirkung* (Vienna: Wiener Volksbuchhandlung, 1947), 4. All translations in this book by Gabriel Kuhn unless noted otherwise.

Acknowledgments

I thank everyone who has provided research material and illustrations for this book, in particular Wolfgang Burghardt from the International Workers and Amateurs in Sports Confederation (*Conféderation Sportive International Travailliste et Amateur*, CSIT) and Elisabeth Boeckl-Klamper from the Documentation Centre of Austrian Resistance (*Dokumentationsarchiv des österreichischen Widerstandes*, DÖW). Special thanks also to the Stockholm Labour Movement Archives and Library (*Arbetarrörelsens arkiv och bibliotek*) whose excellent German-language collection and wonderful staff make it possible to wrap up works like these away from home. Needless to say, the responsibility for the book's contents lies solely with me.

PART I

AUSTROMARXISM, RED VIENNA, AND WORKING-CLASS CULTURE

Gabriel Kuhn

Historical Background

When World War I began with the Austro-Hungarian Empire declaring war on Serbia, the empire contained the territories of modern-day Austria, Hungary, the Czech Republic, Slovakia, Slovenia, Croatia, and Bosnia and Herzegovina, as well as significant parts of modern-day Poland, Romania, and Italy. After the war, the empire's German-speaking part (except for South Tyrol, which went to Italy) became the nation state of Austria that we know today.

The Emperor abdicated on November 11, 1918; the following day, Austria was proclaimed a republic. The First Austrian Republic (as it is referred to today) existed until 1934. It was characterized by strong political tensions between, on the one hand, socialists, mainly organized in the SDAP and affiliated organizations, and, on the other hand, right-wing forces consisting of monarchists, a reactionary clergy, the national bourgeoisie, conservative peasants, Mussolini-admiring fascists, and pan-German-oriented National Socialists. These tensions led to a civil war in February 1934, which saw the right-wing forces victorious. The authoritarian regime established a year earlier was now unchallenged, altered the constitution, and assumed dictatorial powers. This was the beginning of the Austrofascist era.

From the onset, the Austrofascists, who had close ties to Mussolini, were challenged by the National Socialists who had seized power in Germany a year earlier. A Nazi coup attempt in July 1934 failed, but in 1938, the Nazis did seize power when Hitler sent German troops into Austria and made the country a part of the Third Reich.

When World War II ended in 1945, the republic was restored and the history of the Second Austrian Republic, which exists to this day, began.[1]

This is the historical framework in which the following story unfolds.

Austromarxism and Red Vienna

According to Otto Bauer, the term *Austromarxism* stems from the American author Louis Boudin, who used it in 1907 to identify a particular group of Vienna-based socialists.[2] But as a distinct school within Marxist thought, Austromarxism only received recognition in the interwar period when its most prominent figures played leading roles in the SDAP. Much of this recognition was related to Red Vienna, the Austromarxists' most impressive practical showpiece.

Austromarxist theory was almost single-handedly defined by Otto Bauer (1881–1938), the Vienna-born son of a factory owner and vice chairman of the SDAP from 1918 to 1934. Only Max Adler (1873–1937) came close to Bauer in terms of intellectual weight, surprising the socialist world with studies such as *Max Stirner und der moderne Sozialismus* (Max Stirner and Modern Socialism, 1906) and *Demokratie und Rätesystem* (Democracy and the Council System, 1919). Friedrich Adler (1879–1960), the son of the SDAP's founding father and lifelong chairman, Victor Adler (1852–1918; neither of them related to Max), was—like Julius Deutsch (1884–1968)—more important as a representative figure.

Others who are at times identified as Austromarxists had already left Austria by the end of World War I, most notably Karl Kautsky (1854–1938) and Rudolf Hilferding (1877–1941), while the republic's first chancellor Karl Renner (1870–1950),[3] who represented the right wing of the SDAP,

4

had little influence on the school's ideological development and was, in fact, often opposed to it.

Austromarxism distinguished itself by the following features:

■ While, in the wake of the Russian Revolution, there was a clear split between reformist social democrats and revolutionary Marxists in most European countries, the SDAP managed to retain both camps. After the end of the Austro-Hungarian Empire, most of the SDAP's left wing decided not to join the *Kommunistische Partei Österreichs* (Communist Party of Austria, KPÖ), when it was founded in November 1918. As a consequence, the KPÖ remained insignificant throughout the entire interwar period.[4]

Perhaps the strongest blow to the Communists was Friedrich Adler's refusal to join their ranks. In October 1916, Adler had become the most famous representative of the SDAP's left wing after assassinating the Austrian minister-president Karl Stürgkh in protest against the government's warmongering. Yet, when the Austro-Hungarian Empire fell, Adler did not consider the time ripe for revolution. On June 30, 1919, he explained his position at the second National Conference of the Workers' Councils:

> The difference in evaluating the historical situation is that the communists abide by Lenin's and Trotsky's announcement that the world revolution must follow the end of the war, that capitalism's collapse is imminent, and that capitalism cannot recover. We social democrats, however, evaluate things according to economic conditions and laws. It might not be guaranteed that capitalism will recover, but how things will develop depends on the political and economic circumstances of each individual country. The communists believe that the wish for revolution is enough. . . .

But we cannot build our politics on wishes alone. We social democrats say: even if it is indeed our wish that capitalism will never again rule the world, we cannot ignore the facts.[5]

The people joining the KPÖ were so few and inexperienced that even Lenin conceded in 1920 that the party was based on "the illusions that a group professing to communism can become a political force even if they have no support among the masses."[6]

From 1918 on, being a Social Democrat in Austria meant something very different to being a Social Democrat in other European countries. The SDAP remained an unwavering Marxist party when most of Europe's social democracy was moving toward the liberal center (or worse). The Austrian Social Democrats were, in the words of E.J. Hobsbawm, "radical, militant . . . and in any case rejected the sort of social democracy which defines itself essentially as an anti-Bolshevik force."[7]

■ With its radical wing intact, the SDAP styled itself as a "third way" socialism "between reformism and Bolshevism," as the most comprehensive study of Austromarxism, Norbert Leser's *Zwischen Reformismus und Bolschewismus*, suggests in its title. The most referenced nod to Bolshevism can be found in the party platform of 1926—known as the *Linzer Programm* (Linz being Austria's third-biggest city and one of the few industrial centers outside Vienna)—in which the SDAP alludes to the dictatorship of the proletariat. The relevant passage reads as follows:

> The SDAP will govern *by the means of democracy* and it will respect *all democratic obligations*. These obligations imply that the actions of a social democratic government will always be controlled by the majority of a people united under the leadership of the

working class, and that the government always has to account for its actions to this majority. The democratic obligations will allow for the creation of the socialist system under the best possible conditions, that is, the active and unrestrained participation of the masses. However, if the bourgeoisie—by means of economic sabotage, violent rebellion, or conspiracy with foreign counterrevolutionary forces—resists the transformation that a proletarian government is required to implement, then the working class will be forced *to break this resistance by means of a dictatorship.*[8]

The Austromarxist idea of a socialist third way was by no means only a theoretical spook. In 1921, Austromarxist leaders organized a conference in Vienna with representatives from all the European socialist parties refusing to pledge allegiance to either the social democratic Second International (known today as the Socialist International) or the communist Third International (the Comintern). At the conference, the International Working Union of Socialist Parties (IWUSP, in German *Internationale Arbeitsgemeinschaft sozialistischer Parteien*) was founded with the aim to unite both camps. The efforts were in vain, however, not least due to a complete disinterest on the side of the communists. Karl Radek, at the time secretary of the Comintern, derided the IWUSP as the "Two and a Half International."[9] In 1923, the IWUSP-affiliated parties abandoned their diplomatic ambitions and joined the Second International.

The Austromarxist approach was summarized in the phrase "integral socialism," coined by Otto Bauer and based on dialectics:

> It is not enough to bring opposing political ideologies together. . . . The challenge which history poses socialism is rather to unite the social democratic thesis and

the communist antithesis in a new, higher synthesis. As important as the alliance of social democracy and communism is in everyday political struggle, it will not succeed if it cannot overcome both the social democratic and the communist shortcomings in an *integral socialism* that will incorporate both social democracy and communism.[10]

■ Austromarxism was not only a political endeavor but closely linked to the cultural developments in Austria—particularly in Vienna—during the interwar period. Vienna had always been the bastion of the SDAP and the Austromarxists, to the point where historians have called Austromarxism "a Vienna-based phenomenon."[11] This is not entirely true, but it indicates a deep geographical rift that has always characterized Austrian politics, namely that between Vienna plus a few scattered industrial and mining towns on the one hand and the conservative Catholic countryside on the other.

After winning Vienna's May 1919 municipal elections with an absolute majority, the SDAP embarked on an extremely ambitious urban reform program that promised a kind of real-life workers' utopia, including modern housing, universal health care, efficient public transport, extensive social services, a diversity of communal facilities, and a vast network of educational and cultural institutions. In the words of the historian Anson Rabinbach, Red Vienna, as it was soon called, was "the most innovative example of a progressive urban culture and society to be attempted by any major socialist or communist organization outside of Russia."[12] Karl Polanyi described it as "one of the most spectacular cultural triumphs of Western history."[13] Arguably, the Austromarxists came closer to establishing a socialist society without a profound revolutionary rupture than any other political movement.

"Topple Capitalism and Vote for the Social Democrats" SDAP election poster, 1920. *(Private collection)*

Socialists from around the world congregated in Vienna to study the municipal government's policies. The hope that the Austromarxists attached to their experiment was indeed to pave the way for "new human beings," as Max Adler explained in a 1924 book under the same title.[14] Already in 1910, he had stated: "It is no longer paradoxical to assert that socialism is not fundamentally a workers' movement but a cultural movement. The meaning of this cultural development is that socialism will attain a new culture through the working-class movement, that it will bring culture to the workers, and that it will advance through their activities."[15]

In his memoirs, Julius Deutsch described the significance of the Austromarxist experience as follows:

> The workers' movement of this era did not simply see itself as a factor in daily politics. Far from it. It wanted to be more; much more. And in the minds of the workers it was. Its goal was to transform all aspects of society and, as a precondition, recreate the individual. The socialists formed a self-conscious

community that almost had the character of a religious sect. I immersed myself in this closed circle with all my heart. It was my world. I hardly knew another, and I had no desire to get to know another either.[16]

Austromarxism, Red Vienna, and the working-class culture it had created ended with the Austrofascists establishing dictatorial powers in 1934. The SDAP was prohibited and its leading representatives, Deutsch included, forced into exile. (See below for the events of 1934 and the developments leading up to them.) The following observation made by Julius Deutsch in 1960 holds true to this day: "'Austromarxism' . . . gave Austrian socialists an international recognition they never reached again."[17]

After the war, when the SDAP's successor, the *Sozialistische Partei Österreichs* (Socialist Party of Austria, SPÖ[18]), wanted to prove itself as a moderate and mature parliamentarian party, the radical Austromarxist past was swept under the carpet. With Otto Bauer and Max Adler dead, Friedrich Adler remaining in exile, and Deutsch not being granted a leading position in the party, the Austromarxists were soon erased from history. It took until the mid-1960s before there was "a renaissance of interest in Austromarxism"[19] with the Austromarxist experience being studied by Eurocommunist and left-socialist currents searching for credible Marxist positions in the parliamentarian political system of the West. Some of the theoretically most interesting outcomes were based on comparisons between Otto Bauer and Antonio Gramsci.[20]

In 2008, the editors of the volume *Otto Bauer und der Austromarxismus."Integraler Sozialismus" und die heutige Linke* (Otto Bauer and Austromarxism: "Integral Socialism" and Today's Left), which included contributions by over twenty socialist scholars, claimed that the relevance of the Austromarxist approach had not ceased:

For us, two goals are attached to the study of Otto Bauer's work. The first is to remind people of the existence and continuity of Marxist thinking in international social democracy during the interwar period and to make this a reference point for current left-socialist positions in the social democratic and socialist parties of Western Europe. Second, we would like to relate the problems of the international workers' movement that Otto Bauer discussed, as well as the orientations and solutions he proposed, to the enquiries, discussions, and perspectives of the contemporary Left.[21]

The Communist Critique

The bourgeois depiction of the Austromarxists as dangerous "Bolsheviks in sheep's clothing" was predictable and is nothing we want to dwell on here. It is more interesting to consider the critique of other Marxists, especially those who indeed were Bolsheviks.

Most commonly, the Bolsheviks targeted the gap between radical rhetoric and reformist politics that characterized Austromarxism, perhaps reflecting "a specifically Austrian phenomenon, namely the blend of intellectual sharpness and pragmatic fluffiness."[22] Rather than wolves in sheep's clothing, the Austromarxists were considered all bark and no bite.

Leon Trotsky, who regularly used to meet and discuss with leading proponents of the tendency, including Julius Deutsch, while residing in Vienna from 1907 to 1914, remembered them thus:

> It was Hilferding who first introduced me to his friends in Vienna, Otto Bauer, Max Adler, and Karl Renner. They were well-educated people whose knowledge

of various subjects was superior to mine. I listened with intense and, one might almost say, respectful interest to their conversation in the "Central" cafe. But very soon I grew puzzled. These people were not revolutionaries. Moreover, they represented the type that was farthest from that of the revolutionary. This expressed itself in everything, in their approach to subjects, in their political remarks and psychological appreciations, in their self-satisfaction—not self-assurance, but self-satisfaction . . . . I was surprised to find that these educated Marxists were absolutely incapable of applying Marx's method as soon as they came to the big problems of politics, especially its revolutionary turns.[23]

Lenin blew into the same horn: "Friedrich Adler and Otto Bauer can twist and squirm as much as they like, use up reams of paper and make endless speeches, but they cannot get away from the fact that *in practice* they absolutely fail to understand the dictatorship of the proletariat and Soviet power, that *in practice* they are petty-bourgeois democrats . . . that *in practice* they are, at best, puppets in the hands of the bourgeoisie, and, at worst, direct hirelings of the bourgeoisie."[24]

Austrian socialist historians have approached the same problem from a different angle:

The fear of partition was a trauma for Austromarxism. Its consequence was to avoid everything that could possibly lead to a split. Such subjects were taboo. The formation of factions, crucial votes, and heated discussions within the party threatened its spirit and were therefore avoided at all costs. However, it was not only difficult questions and forceful directions that one shied away from but even simple discomfort.

> The line chosen within the party was always the one
> of least resistance. Of course, this meant none of the
> pressures and dangers that inevitably come from
> audacious and critical decisions. But it also meant
> the loss of all opportunities that such decisions bring.
> In the end, those caught in the vicious circle of party
> ideology no longer found a way to escape it.[25]

The Austromarxists' defense against these allega-
tions was typical for their intellectual prowess. Otto Bauer
assumed the role of dialectic philosopher: "What appears to
the dogmatist as halfheartedness, as inner contradiction, as
an exasperating 'on the one hand this—on the other hand
that,' is nothing but the dialectical method," he claimed in
his 1936 work with the tragically prophetic title *Zwischen
zwei Weltkriegen?* (Between Two World Wars?).[26] However,
what in laymen's terms was simple indecision ran through
Austromarxist history like a red thread.

It started with the party's reaction to the council republic proclaimed in Hungary on March 21, 1919. The Hungarian
revolutionaries issued a call for the SDAP to follow their
example, but without result. The SDAP responded with an
open letter in its newspaper, *Arbeiter-Zeitung* (The Workers'
Journal), stating matter-of-factly: "You have called upon us
to follow your example—from our hearts, we wish we could,
but right now this is not possible." The reason cited was
Austria's dependence on the Entente[27] regarding food deliv-
eries. The text concluded: "All our wishes are with you. With
warm hearts we follow the events and hope that *the cause of
socialism* will prevail."[28]

At the time, Julius Deutsch was minister for defense.
Certainly to his credit, he looked the other way when radical
Austrian workers delivered weapons to Hungary. He also
sent an envoy to advise the German minister for defense
Gustav Noske against employing reactionary soldiers—the

infamous Free Corps—in his military efforts to crush radical workers' uprisings across Germany.[29] Still, the SDAP's reaction to the developments in Hungary—where the council republic lasted for about four months—revealed a hesitance in taking political risks that would define their politics all the way to 1934.

Victor Serge remembers the period somewhat melodramatically:

> *If only.* . . . If only a Red Austria had joined with the Hungarian Soviets, would not troubled Bohemia, and then Germany, have followed their example? Revolution was maturing in Italy during this same period. But perhaps it was already too late. . . . If only the Social-Democrats of Austria had had a little of the impassioned energy of the Bolsheviks of Russia! All they ever did was to sip sweet white wine in the operetta-land of the Blue Danube, while the Bolsheviks were tramping in chains along Siberian highways.[30]

The refusal to proclaim a council republic also provoked clashes with communists on the home front. A botched communist coup in June 1919 led to twenty dead workers. Deutsch put the blame on the KPÖ, stating: "The responsibility lies with those who, through mad agitation, fed a few thousand people the absurd idea that the violent act of a small minority could force a dictatorship on the majority of the people."[31] How mad the agitation and how absurd the idea were is difficult to assess, but even Karl Radek called the events a proof for the "cretinism of coup tactics."[32]

Ironically, one of the reasons why the SDAP drew strict boundaries between itself and the communists was the relative radicalness of its own line. Retaining most of its left wing, it seemed that only adventurists, lunatics, and *agents provocateurs* would feel a need to organize independently. There was also a strong sense that the Austrian communists were used as pawns by foreign—mainly Hungarian, but also Russian—forces. Yet there were also reconciling tones. In 1921, Deutsch summed up his relationship to the communists thus: "The whole time I did the utmost to prove to the communist workers and soldiers that the social democrats' revolutionary will was no less honest than theirs. Even if we had different views on the political questions of the day, it seemed important to remember that we shared the same goals. Even during the most critical of times I tried not to lose personal connection with the communists. They were misguided proletarians, but they were still proletarians."[33]

Workers' Militias

The SDAP founded the *Republican Schutzbund* in 1923 as a network of workers' militias responding to the ever-increasing threat posed by reactionary paramilitaries formed under the banner of the *Heimwehr* (Militant Home Defense), which combined Catholic conservatives, monarchists, and fascists.

In the first issue of the organization's monthly journal, *Der Schutzbund*, Deutsch, who had been elected chairman, described the organization thus: "The violent acts of monarchism and fascism have not discouraged the Austrian workers. To the contrary: they have motivated them to organize in response. A network of marshals, loosely formed in the beginning, has developed into a much more rigid organization: the Republican Schutzbund. The Schutzbund's goal can be summarized in a few words: *it wants to save the working class from the violent acts of monarchism and fascism; it wants to defend democracy and the republic*."[34]

The historical record of the Schutzbund equals that of the SDAP: tough talk was rarely backed up by tough action. For years, the Schutzbund focused on tactics of de-escalation, never actively confronting the reactionary paramilitaries. The reason given was always the same, namely to avoid a civil war.[35] This despite the *Linzer Programm* stating clearly: "If,

DER SCHUTZBUND

NR.7.·3.JAHRGANG
WIEN, JULI 1926

FESTNUMMER DER MONATSSCHRIFT DES
REPUBLIKANISCHEN SCHUTZBUNDES AN:
LÄSSLICH DES ERSTEN REICHSORDNER:
TAGES ◇ 11.JULI 1926 ◇ WIEN

Der Schutzbund cover from July 1926. *(Private collection)*

despite all efforts by the social democratic workers, a bourgeois counterrevolution succeeds in crushing democracy,
the working class has no choice but to conquer state power
in a civil war."[36]

Two dates are of particular significance for the Schutzbund's reluctance to engage its enemy in a decisive battle.

The first is July 15, 1927, a defining day in Austrian history.

On January 30, 1927, two people—a disabled war veteran and a seven-year-old boy—were killed when right-wing militias opened fire on a SDAP march in the small town of Schattendorf, Burgenland. This was far from the first such incident. Fascist attacks on socialists had increased in recent years, with the police and the justice system usually turning a blind eye. But when the Schattendorf killers were acquitted by a jury in the Vienna regional court in July, it was the straw that broke the camel's back. Thousands of workers poured into the Vienna streets, embarked on a spontaneous march on the Palace of Justice (*Justizpalast*), seat of the Supreme Court, and set it on fire. For many workers, this would have been the perfect opportunity for the Schutzbund to demonstrate its strength, come to their support, and make it clear that neither the reactionary violence nor the political and judicial powers protecting it would stand. Instead, the Schutzbund leaders hesitated to deploy their units, fearing, as always, an escalation. Only when a police assault on the demonstration was underway were Schutzbund units sent to the site, but they could no longer make it through the enraged masses and were even attacked by some infuriated protesters. When the police did launch its assault, eighty-four workers died in a hail of bullets. Since some protesters fired back, five policemen died as well.

The event proved traumatic for Austria's working class and gave an enormous boost to the reactionaries. The historian Franz West contends: "Fascist provocations, terrorist attacks, assaults, and assassinations increased, and the systematic fascistization of public life began. The Social Democrats, at the time still strong, retreated in the face

An die Bevölkerung des II. Bezirkes!

In letzter Zeit suchte das gesamte Häuflein Wiener Haken-kreuzler unseren Bezirk auf, um hier die sozialdemokratische Arbeiterschaft anzupöbeln.

Obwohl sie immer wieder mit einer tüchtigen Tracht Prügel nach Hause geschickt werden und jedesmal bei der Polizei Schutz suchen, versuchen sie dennoch an mehreren Tagen in der Woche die Arbeiterschaft unseres Bezirkes zu provozieren.

Männer und Frauen! Wir werden diesem Treiben einen Riegel vor-schieben und veranstalten am

Sonntag, den 16. Oktober 1932 um 10ʰ vorm. auf dem Sportplatz der Sport-vereinigung der Städt. E-Werke IX, Wien,

II. Engerthstr., neben dem Kühllagerhaus der Stadt Wien, eine

Antifaschistische Kundgebung

unter der Parole

Zerschlagt das Hakenkreuz

Es sprechen:

Nationalrat Dr. Julius Deutsch
Gemeinderat Herman Fischer
Gemeinderat Ernst Papanek

anschließend: Übergabe einer Sturmfahne an die Wehrsportler der soz. Arbeiterjugend II und Angelobung der Alarmabtei-lung des Republikanischen Schutzbundes II.

Um 9 Uhr vormittags findet ein Staffettenlauf „Quer durch die Leopoldstadt" statt; Start: Praterstr. 25, Ziel: E-Werk-Platz.

Einlaß auf den E-Werk-Platz nur mit dem Antifaschistischen Kampfabzeichen.

Erscheint in Massen!

Die Abzeichen sind à 10 Groschen im Parteisekretariat, II. Praterstraße 25 und bei den Vertrauenspersonen erhältlich.

Republikanischer Schutzbund II.   Verband der soz. Arbeiterjugend II.

Republican Schutzbund announcement of an antifascist demonstration under the slogan "Smash the Swastika!" in Vienna, October 1932. Julius Deutsch is listed among the speakers. *(Private collection)*

of these aggressions and thereby encouraged the fascists and their backers to step up the aggression even more."[37] This is when the foundations for Austrofascism were laid.

According to Norbert Leser, Austria's most prominent social democratic historian, "the way from July 15, 1927, to . . . February 1934 was a logical and consistent one."[38]

Four months after the event, Deutsch published a defiant explanation for the Schutzbund's actions (or lack thereof) in the organization's journal: "If we, today, some weeks after July 15, revisit the events before our inner eyes and evaluate them, we cannot come to a different conclusion than the one we had reached on that very day: not deploying the Schutzbund was the only means to prevent an outcome even worse than the one we have seen. Had the Schutzbund, as some wanted, struck back against the police, the waves of the bloodiest civil war would have come over our country. Everyone in a position of responsibility had to prevent such a catastrophe."[39]

Deutsch's statement omits a few crucial facts. The republic had been threatened long before July 15, 1927, and if that had not been clear, the police's response that day left no doubt. The time for the inevitability of a civil war to save the republic, as proclaimed in the *Linzer Programm*, had come. But neither the SDAP nor the Schutzbund leadership took measures to meet this inevitability. In light of this, statements by Deutsch such as "it is crystal clear that the proletariat . . . cannot fight with democratic means alone when its class enemy has long left these grounds"[40] and "the bourgeoisie forces its law upon us, and that is, unfortunately, the law of violence"[41] seem indeed confusing or even deceptive.

The second date of great importance for the Schutzbund history was March 15, 1933. After a violation of protocol had led to the suspension of parliament in early March, the members of the opposition, including the SDAP delegates, wanted to reconvene in the parliament building on March 15. They were hindered from entering by the police upon orders of Chancellor Engelbert Dollfuss, who had been heading a center-right coalition since May 1932. This effectively meant an end to parliamentarism in Austria. A change of the republican constitution only seemed a matter of time. Even at this point, the Schutzbund did not intervene. Instead, it continued to cite the necessity of diplomacy, although the futility of diplomatic means had long been proven. March 15, 1933, would have been ideal for an uprising backed by the proletarian masses. A year later—after the defeat in the civil war of February 1934—Otto Bauer admitted at least as much:

> The conditions for a successful struggle were never as good as on March 15. . . . The working masses were waiting for an order to strike back. . . . The government's military forces were much weaker at the time than in February 1934. In March 1933, we might have had a chance to win, but we shied away from the struggle. We still believed that a peaceful solution could be reached through negotiations. . . . We avoided the struggle because we wanted to spare the country the catastrophe of a bloody civil war. Eleven months later, the civil war came anyway, but for us under much less favorable circumstances. We had made a mistake; the most fatal of our mistakes.[42]

The KPÖ was prohibited in May 1933 and the SDAP's newspaper *Arbeiter-Zeitung* in January 1934. Shortly thereafter, the government began its final assault on the Schutzbund, which had also been prohibited in May 1933 but continued as an underground organization. Far-reaching searches for weapons were planned and executed. When one of the Schutzbund strongholds in Linz, the Hotel Schiff, was searched on February 12, the Linz Schutzbund leader Richard Bernaschek commanded his units to resist. The ensuing armed struggle soon spread to other parts of the country, leaving the SDAP and the national Schutzbund leaders no choice but to react. Otto Bauer and Julius Deutsch called for a general strike to support the Schutzbund, but few workers

Rudolf Kunz was one of the Schutzbund fighters who
died during the assault on the Hotel Schiff in Linz.
(Dokumentationsarchiv des österreichischen Widerstandes)

heeded the call. Some Schutzbund units also refused to join
the struggle. Others were waiting for arms and instructions
at designated meeting points, but never received any due to
poor communication. After all of the frustrations of recent
years and lost chances, the Austrian workers were demoralized and had lost trust in their leadership.

Most of the fighting that did take place in Vienna
focused on the *Gemeindebauten*, huge municipal tenement
complexes for workers, such as the Karl-Marx-Hof, erected
by the SDAP and among Red Vienna's most prestigious pro-
jects. But the Schutzbund units stood no chance against the
combined forces of the army, police, and Heimwehr. The
workers who fought back became the tragic protagonists of
an ill-fated antifascist rebellion that came too late and was
doomed to fail. The Austrian Civil War was over in a matter
of days.

Seen from a positive angle, the Austrian Civil War was
a heroic working-class struggle against fascism. Unlike
the workers in Italy or Germany, the Austrian proletariat
did not give in to fascist rule without a fight. Seen from a

The Karl-Marx-Hof after the February clashes.
(*Dokumentationsarchiv des österreichischen Widerstandes*)

negative angle, it was an act of desperation whose chance for success had long been undermined by poor leadership. The Hungarian revolutionary Ilona Duczynska, who lived in Vienna at the time, reached the following harsh verdict in her book *Workers in Arms: The Austrian Schutzbund and the Civil War of 1934*:

"A political leadership lacking any positive aim, any orientation on revolutionary statesmanship; broad masses whose enthusiasm had given way to apathy; paramilitary troops with no roots in the masses of the people; a chief of staff [Alexander Eifler] who, together with his staff, allowed himself to be captured before the battle; no travesty of that 'odd kind of trinity' of war (including civil war) . . . could have turned out to be more shattering."[43]

Duczynska also pointed out that Deutsch, trained in the standing Imperial and Royal Army of Austria-Hungary, was not the right man to lead a militia organization.[44] Over the years, there had been intense debates about the right tactics for the Schutzbund between Deutsch and the chief of staff Alexander Eifler on the on hand, and the experienced general Theodor Körner (later the first president of the Second Austrian Republic) on the other. Körner was convinced that the Schutzbund could never succeed in a conventional military confrontation with the government and that the strict militarization of the Schutzbund was therefore inappropriate. Instead, he proposed clandestine tactics that, according to Ilona Duczynska, "today are known to us as modern guerrilla warfare."[45] Other critics of the Schutzbund's militarization stressed that it undermined workers' self-initiative, contradicted the cultural ideals of Austromarxism, and turned the organization into a policing force of the workers rather than a fighting force against the bourgeoisie. However, Deutsch and Eifler were unperturbed and insisted that a strong fighting force had to emulate the military. According to Duczynska, "in the autumn of 1927 the main point was to streamline, discipline, and depoliticize the Schutzbund."[46] This is seconded by the Austrian historian Karl Haas: "Of a working class in arms, of a proletarian militia, all that remained as a sorry remnant was the party soldiery under appointed leaders."[47]

Other historians have also claimed that, despite all this, the Schutzbund would still have had a chance to succeed in February 1934 had the leadership only acted fast enough in the earliest phases of the struggle. In his personal account of the events, the conservative government's chief of press, Eduard Ludwig, maintained the following:

"The first district, seat of the government and of all the administrative offices, remained practically undefended for hours. Had the Republican Schutzbund, immediately after the decision for action was taken, carried out a serious attack, there can be no doubt that it could have taken control of the first district and thereby the entire city of Vienna."[48]

According to Deutsch, such a possibility never existed:

"It became clear during the first hours of the struggle that our forces were weaker than those of the government.

23

Barricade in front of one of Vienna's Workers' Libraries.
(Dokumentationsarchiv des österreichischen Widerstandes)

Furthermore, the government had the advantage of the inner line because it had already occupied the inner city and all of its important buildings days before. It was not possible to force them from there. All of the attempts that were made failed."[49]

Today, it seems impossible to determine who was right, and it would not change the facts: the fighting left close to two hundred workers and over one hundred security forces and government sympathizers dead; nine Schutzbund leaders were executed and hundreds of members arrested or driven into exile. Meanwhile, the Austrofascists had the perfect excuse to change the constitution and cement their dictatorial rule.

Otto Bauer and Julius Deutsch escaped across the border to Czechoslovakia when the fighting neared its end. Had they been arrested in Austria, their execution would have been certain. Tragically enough, out of the many Schutzbund fighters who accepted an offer of asylum in the Soviet Union, at least 197 were executed during Stalin's purges. Gustav Deutsch, Julius's son, was among them. He was sentenced to death as a Trotskyist spy on June 14, 1938, and executed the same day. In 1956, he was rehabilitated. His wife Agnes spent eight years in the Gulag and died in Moscow in 1976.

Following the civil war, all workers' organizations in Austria, including the SDAP, were dissolved. While Bauer and Deutsch founded the *Auslandsbüro der österreichischen Sozialdemokraten* (Foreign Bureau of Austrian Social Democrats, ALÖS) in Czechoslovakia, the *Revolutionäre Sozialisten* (Revolutionary Socialists, RS) established themselves as a radical underground successor to the SDAP in Austria. In March 1938, when Nazi rule—even more ruthless than the Austrofascist one—made underground organizing near impossible, the RS leadership fled abroad and united with ALÖS to form the *Auslandsvertretung der österreichischen Sozialisten* (Foreign Representation of Austrian Socialists, AVOES).

Meanwhile, the ranks of the KPÖ—which kept organizing in the country despite all the difficulties and dangers—had swelled with disillusioned Social Democrats who had no means or will to flee the country. The Communists stood for some of the most effective underground resistance against the Nazis during the war. This brought them seats in the Austrian parliament for the first time in the inaugural postwar elections of 1945. They defended their seats until 1959 before once again disappearing into oblivion.[50] The Schutzbund itself existed for another two years as an "autonomous communist movement,"[51] but was then "swallowed by the parties."[52]

Workers' Sport

The workers' sport movement emerged in the late nineteenth century on both sides of the Atlantic with workers' sports clubs and associations founded in several European and Latin American countries. The German-speaking world soon emerged as the center of the movement, however, which reflected the overall strength of its working-class institutions.

In Austria, the first workers' gymnastics club was founded in Vienna in 1891. By 1894, it had adopted the name *Allgemeiner Turnverein* (General Gymnastics Club) and various sports were played. Similar clubs were founded around the country during the following years, and in 1910 they united in the *Österreichischer Arbeiter-Turnerbund* (Austrian Workers' Gymnastics League), counting seventy thousand members at the time of its formation. In 1919, the organization was renamed *Verband der Arbeiter- und Soldatensportvereinigungen* (Association of Workers' and Soldiers' Sports Clubs), and in 1924, *Arbeiterbund für Sport und Körperkultur in Österreich* (Workers' League for Sport and Body Culture in Austria, ASKÖ). The sports practiced included gymnastics, cycling, hiking, swimming, skiing, football, handball, judo, and even sports almost exclusively associated with the bourgeoisie such as tennis.

Early on, many socialist parties across Europe eyed workers' sport with caution, seeing it as a distraction from the proletariat's political duties, that is, organizing in the party and the union. With time, however, the party and union leaders understood the importance of cultural elements in the political struggle—or, at least, they understood that many young workers got more excited about joining a sports club than about attending a political meeting.

With the Austromarxists being at the forefront of the proletarian cultural struggle, it is not surprising that ASKÖ became the world's biggest national workers' sports association relative to the size of the country's population. At its peak, ASKÖ had around three hundred thousand members.

Julius Deutsch's involvement in the politics of sports started early. The first time he met the SDAP chairman Victor Adler, it was because Deutsch wanted to secure Adler's support in forming a football team at a workers' club he attended. This was in 1898 (Deutsch being only fourteen years old), at a time when workers' sport was still mainly met

Workers' athletes pose together with Schutzbund members for a photograph in Ebensee, Upper Austria. *(Archiv Zeitgeschichte Museum Ebensee)*

with skepticism among socialist leaders. In Adler's office, Deutsch explained to the don of Austrian social democracy that physical training was as important for the working class as educational pursuits. Adler encouraged Deutsch to write down his thoughts and had them published in the *Arbeiter-Zeitung*. It was the beginning of Adler's lifelong promotion of Julius.

In 1926, Deutsch became ASKÖ's president and one year later assumed presidency of the Socialist Workers' Sport International (SWSI), founded in 1920. At its peak, the SWSI had about two million members hailing from over twenty countries, including the United States and Palestine.

At the heart of the workers' sport movement stood the fight against individualism, competitiveness, and commercialism. The values promoted were community, sportsmanship, and health. Running competitions were replaced by walking tours in the countryside; swimming races by lifesaving courses; duels in wrestling by collective workouts; "tournaments" by "sports festivals"; "national teams" by "federations"; "performance mania" by "physical exercise."[53] In

SPEZIAL-
HAUS
FÜR
JEDEN SPORT

SPEZIAL-
HAUS
FÜR SPORT-
BEKLEIDUNG

TELEPHON NR.:
A - 31 - 0 - 40

TELEGRAMME:
-SASI- WIEN

SPORTHAUS »SASI«
WIEN, 5. BEZIRK, MARGARETENGÜRTEL NR. 126

Advertisement for the SWSI sports boutique in Vienna (SASI was the organization's German acronym). *(Private collection)*

1933, the Austrian Social Democrat Hans Gastgeb summed up the goals of workers' sport thus: "For the worker athlete, mass sport and political education are one. Sport is not practiced for distraction, but as a necessary means to shape a proletariat that is mentally and physically prepared to overthrow capitalism and prevail against the reactionary forces in politics, economics, and culture."[54]

Workers' sport organizations were not only an essential part of the proletarian culture of their time, but they also granted the average worker more influence than most other workers' organizations. The historian Robert F. Wheeler states: "In fact, there was probably no other component of organized labour in which rank-and-file interaction was greater. . . . International congresses might pass resolutions about understanding and solidarity but labour sports could, and frequently did, provide practical manifestations of these ideas."[55]

Many sports events were organized under the auspices of the SWSI. The biggest were the Workers' Olympics. The first were arranged in Germany in 1925: the winter games

"Proletarians from around the world unite in sport!" Closing Parade at the 1931 Workers' Olympics in Vienna. *(ASKÖ/CSIT)*

were held in Schreiberhau/Szklarska Poręba (today Poland), the summer games in Frankfurt. The guidebook of the Frankfurt games explained the intentions behind them:

> The bourgeois Olympic Games will always be marred by the "unspirit" of nationalism, since the capitalist world knows nothing about true reconciliation. Our Olympics are based on understanding and openness between the peoples. In our Olympics, nations do not compete *against* each other, but athletes from all countries compete *with* each other as comrades. . . . We all have the same enemy: capitalism, which has created nationalism and continues to foster it. We do not give laurel wreaths to nations, and we do not fly their flags; instead, we come together as brothers and sisters under the flag of socialism.

The second, and biggest, Workers' Olympics took place in Austria in 1931. The winter games were held in Mürzzuschlag, the summer games in Vienna. The number of

"Fascism will never score a goal in Red Vienna. Worker footballers vouch for it." Banner at the 1931 Workers' Olympics in Vienna. *(ASKÖ/CSIT)*

participants had risen to about twenty-five thousand. During the opening ceremony, four thousand workers enacted the history of the working class; the performance ended with an oversized capitalist's head breaking into pieces. As in Frankfurt, no national flags were flown and no national anthems played.

Unfortunately, the international workers' sport movement was marred by a rift. In 1921, the Red Sport International (RSI) had been founded as a rival organization to the SWSI. The RSI never really thrived outside of the Soviet Union; Czechoslovakia and Norway were the only two countries where RSI affiliates could challenge their SWSI counterparts. Nonetheless, the conflict between the two organizations came to a head before the first Workers' Olympics in Germany and RSI-affiliated athletes were not allowed to participate. The ban was upheld six years later in Austria. As notes from SWSI meetings show, Deutsch was very adamant about enforcing it. The lenient attitude he had expressed toward Austrian communists a few years earlier seemed to have disappeared on the international level. At the 1927 SWSI congress in Helsinki, he declared: "According to us, the development of the economic conditions cannot be accelerated by acts of violence and terror; socialism cannot be realized with a bayonet. What has been achieved in Russia is not socialism, it is Sovietism. In any case, Western and Central Europe needs a different tactic; a bloody dictatorship of the proletariat would lead to the people's downfall."[56]

The international workers' sport movement collapsed in the 1930s. In Germany, the Nazis prohibited all workers' sports associations after gaining power in March 1933. In Austria, the fascist regime under Engelbert Dollfuss did the same one year later.[57] With the centers of the movement wiped out and a war looming, workers' sport struggled to survive. The Third Workers' Olympics in 1937 were still held in Janské Lázně, Czechoslovakia (winter games), and Antwerp, Belgium (summer games), but despite both SWSI- and RSI-affiliated athletes participating together for the first time, there were only half as many athletes as there had been in Austria six years earlier. Both the SWSI and the RSI dissolved soon thereafter.[58]

Wehrsport

When the fascist threat arose in Europe in the 1920s, workers' movement leaders explicitly linked workers' sport to antifascist resistance. Julius Deutsch was one of the driving forces behind this development. In Austria, the Republican Schutzbund was made an official part of ASKÖ, and *Wehrsport* ("paramilitary sport" is probably the best English translation, while "defense sport" is more literal) became an important part of ASKÖ's program. Wehrsport contained cross-country running, shooting sports, martial arts, and other disciplines connected to military training.[59] As president of the SWSI, Deutsch campaigned hard for establishing Wehrsport

Genossen, werdet wehrhaft!

Der **Sport** entfaltet jene **körperlichen, moralischen** und **geistigen** Kräfte, die die Arbeiterklasse zu ihrem wirtschaftlichen und kulturellen **Aufstieg** braucht

Jiu-Jitsu

die waffenlose, aber wirkungsvollste Verteidigungsmethode **stählt den Körper, weckt den Mut, erhöht das Selbstgefühl.** Tretet daher bei dem

Arbeiter-Jiu-Jitsu-Klub

Anmeldungen im Sekretariat des Klubs, Wien, 5. Bezirk, Rechte Wienzeile 95, I. Stock, von 15 bis 19 Uhr (außer Samstag und Sonntag)

Einschreibgebühr S 1·—, Kursbeitrag für Ordner monatlich S 2·—, für sonstige Parteimitglieder (Frauen und Männer) S 4·—

"Comrades, Defend Yourselves!" Call for workers to join Vienna's Workers' Jujitsu Club. *(Private collection)*

internationally. At the 1927 SWSI congress, the following resolution was passed:

> In its fight against the proletariat, the capitalist class uses fascist means of attack against democratic and republican forms of government. It employs armed gangs in order to intimidate the workers. . . . The working class can only defend itself successfully if it creates its own defense units. . . . As organizations fostering the physical strength of the proletariat, the task of the workers' sport organizations of all countries is to support these defense units by all means possible. . . . In countries where such units already exist, the workers' sports associations must cooperate with them. There needs to be mutual support.[60]

Deutsch, who stated in his memoirs that "strengthening the body through sports helped me a lot in my military career,"[61] was convinced that sports would help workers to be good soldiers: "The socialist workers' sport movement is a big, global arsenal. It forms and structures the masses, which shall become an army that paves the way to socialism. We can declare with deep satisfaction that more and more people

Der Wehrsport
Eine Anleitung zur Erlernung und Ausübung des Wehrsportes

Herausgegeben von der Zentralleitung des Republikanischen Schutzbundes

Wien 1929

Druck: „Vorwärts" Wien V, Rechte Wienzeile 97

Cover of a Wehrsport manual, edited by the central command of the Republican Schutzbund in 1929. *(Private collection)*

understand the close connection between sports and the proletarian liberation struggle, especially within the SWSI. But also the socialist politicians and unionists increasingly realize that workers' sport is one of the strongest sources of power for the entire working-class movement."[62]

The Schutzbund recruited heavily from workers' sports clubs. Deutsch saw the tasks of the workers' militias and of workers' sport intrinsically linked: "There was a time in the SWSI when many sports were practiced only for sport's sake. Today, practicing sports has become a means to strengthen the proletariat, a means to raise its ability and its passion to fight. This is why the sport organizations and the proletarian defense units need to be linked as closely as possible."[63]

In the eyes of the historian Helmut Gruber, however, this approach led to an "emphasis on discipline to the point of militarization," the outcome being that "a socialist cultural movement was turned into a reserve army in the class struggle,"[64] a critique that echoes Ilona Duczynska's perception of the Schutzbund.

Workers' Sobriety

If the workers' sport movement is largely forgotten, this applies even more so to the workers' temperance movement. When workerists today insist that drinking has always been a part of proletarian culture, they forget that the fight against drinking has always been a part of proletarian culture, too. Already nineteenth-century workers' movements, from the British Chartists to the American Knights of Labor, rallied against alcohol as a means to keep the working classes pacified and to rechannel their hard-earned wages into the capitalists' pockets.

In Europe, the connections between the temperance movement and the workers' movement date back to 1890 when the *Sozialdemokratische Partei der Schweiz* (Social Democratic Party of Switzerland) urged its members to join the newly founded *Internationale Verein zur Bekämpfung des Alkoholgenusses* (International Club to Combat Alcohol Consumption). Switzerland—with figureheads such as the prominent socialist doctor Fritz Brupbacher—remained a center of the socialist struggle for sobriety for a long time,

"Workers, follow the example!" Poster by the German Workers' Temperance League. (*Private collection*)

but the debates soon spread far beyond its borders. Socialist tendencies advocating sobriety became a strong part of the socialist agenda in various European countries. In the Soviet Union, there were extensive (albeit largely unsuccessful) antialcohol campaigns throughout the 1930s; anarchists from Russia to the Netherlands to Spain argued against drink;[65] and several national workers' temperance associations were founded.

Similar to ASKÖ, the Austrian *Arbeiter-Abstinentenbund* (Workers' Temperance League, AAB, founded in 1905) was one of the biggest and most influential relative to the country's size. While Social Democratic leaders in Germany did argue strongly against the devastating effects of liquor on the working class ("Liquor, that is the enemy!" is a quote attributed to Karl Kautsky[66]), they were much more reluctant in their condemnation of beer and wine, which were seen as important ingredients of workers socializing in inns and taverns, an activity that, in turn, was seen as essential for workers organizing.[67] In Austria, the situation was different, as pretty much all of the leading socialists supported the struggle for sobriety. In the list of books and pamphlets published by the AAB, we not only find Julius Deutsch among the authors but also Otto Bauer and Victor Adler—the latter even with a *Gesammelte Reden und Schriften zur Alkoholfrage* (Collected Speeches and Texts on the Question of Alcohol) edition.

Deutsch writes in his memoirs that "a new chapter of his life" started with encountering the workers' temperance movement in the year 1900: "In the spring of 1900, two young Viennese physicians, Dr. Richard Fröhlich and Dr. Rudolf Wlassak, had started to propagate total sobriety among Vienna's workers. They went from meeting to meeting, followed by a group of passionate disciples. The two doctors complemented each other superbly, and we youngsters did not know whom we should admire more."[68]

Fröhlich also made international headlines when he voiced socialist convictions at the largely bourgeois IX International Congress Against Alcoholism in Bremen, Germany, in 1903. He declared that "we antialcoholists must support the efforts of the workers to organize themselves politically and in unions for better wages, better working

Advertisement for publications of the Austrian Workers' Temperance League. (*Private collection*)

conditions, better education, and so on," concluding that "not welfare from above helps the workers but whatever enables them to create a humane existence by their own doing."[69]

While it is undeniable that the workers' temperance movement showed parallels to the moralistic and puritan temperance movements of bourgeois and religious coating, Fröhlich's comments reveal a significant difference: the focus lay not on individual ethical conduct, but on the social role of alcohol and its relation to political organizing and struggle. Otto Bauer made this very clear when explaining his membership in the AAB:

"I don't consider the fight against alcoholism necessary because it harms the health of the individual, but because it harms the workers' movement by demoralizing, corrupting, and bourgeoisifying many good workers who could be great representatives of the workers' movement otherwise. Anyone has the right to harm his own health if he considers the indulgence in certain pleasures worth it; but nobody has the right to encourage indulging in pleasures that hamper the development of the workers' movement by rendering thousands of good comrades incapable of doing their duty."[70]

Julius Deutsch's embrace of the temperance movement might have its roots in childhood experiences as the son of an innkeeper. In his memoirs, Deutsch relates the following story: "In our inn, it was sometimes very lively. I remember terrible fights. Once, a young peasant boy was stabbed with a knife. When he was carried away, covered in blood, his brother led the crowd crying and moaning; this image left a deep impression on me. Afterwards, I heard people say that the boys had had too much to drink. From that point on, I felt a deep aversion to drunkenness."[71]

Deutsch's parallel involvement in the workers' sport movement and the workers' temperance movement was no personal idiosyncrasy. The ties between both movements were strong. A list of SWSI principles contained in the minutes of the 1927 SWSI congress includes the following statement: "Workers' sport must fight against alcohol, which is an enemy of socialist society."[72] Almost all workers' sport declarations include similar pronouncements, and

"Workers, avoid alcohol!" Banner at the 1925 Workers' Olympics in Frankfurt. *(Private collection)*

photographs from the Workers' Olympics in Frankfurt and Vienna show big antialcohol banners.

In Germany, the Social Democratic member of parliament Carl Schreck praised the role of workers' sport in the fight against alcoholism during a 1929 speech at the Social Democrats' party convention: "It has been said that sport all too easily provides an excuse to turn one's back on the fulfillment of socialist obligations, to turn one's back on *political activity*. I may point out that it is much easier to get athletes interested and engaged in the socialist movement than workers who don't do anything but drowning their sorrows in alcohol."[73]

The hope for sport combating alcoholism went beyond workers simply doing sports instead of going to the inn. The hope was that by doing sports they would change their spirit and that it would become easier to withstand the lure of alcohol. In the November 1925 issue of *Der Schutzbund*, the Marxist philosopher Theodor Hartwig wrote: "The athlete abstains from alcohol because he knows that it would affect his performance negatively; but—and this is much more important—the worker who has been disciplined by sports can also abstain from alcohol because his will has been strengthened and he does not give in to temptation."[74]

That Deutsch held on to his beliefs even in exile is confirmed by a short article he contributed to *Der Weckruf* (The Wakeup Call), the journal of the Czechoslovakian Workers' Temperance League, in 1936:

> Worker athletes! You must have heard the saying, "A thinking worker doesn't drink, and a drinking workers doesn't think." It should be taken to heart by all workers, but it contains a particular truth for the worker athlete. Practicing sports means to overcome inner and outer obstacles. It is the victory of the *will* over the *idleness* innate to man. A true athlete knows that his most important quality is not physical ability but the right mental attitude.
>
> Alcohol paralyzes the will. The energy necessary for great athletic performance is reduced by it. This means that for athletic reasons alone alcohol should not belong to an athlete's life. But the worker athlete is not only an athlete, he is also a worker. He must live up to this role as well. He must fight for a better future for the working people, and he carries the responsibility to help shape this future, which will replace the miseries of the existing order with a higher form of existence.
>
> As a soldier for socialism and a fighter for freedom and peace, the worker athlete requires first and foremost the inner strength necessary to persist in the difficult struggles of our time. Clarity and sobriety, discipline and levelheadedness, holy enthusiasm and a will to make sacrifices: these are the qualities that form the socialist struggle. Does it need any proof that such qualities can only prosper in minds not clouded by alcohol?

> Those who are serious about the struggle for a
> more beautiful future for mankind, those who are
> willing to dedicate all of their power to a higher social
> order, those cannot make any other choice but to
> abstain from alcohol, this dangerous enemy of per-
> sonal worth and of a free and dignified humanity.[75]

The AAB was prohibited in 1934. Like the international
workers' sport movement, the international workers' temperance movement collapsed during World War II. Demands
for sobriety were only upheld by elitist organizations such as
the Internationale Sozialistische Kampfbund (International
Socialist Militant League) whose leader Leonard Nelson
maintained that "only a sober worker can be a reliable ally
in the class struggle."[76] While some of the former workers'
sport organizations were at least nominally resurrected, the
workers' temperance movement never regained any significance after the end of the war.[77]

Unsurprisingly, the only country where some connection between the workers' movement and the temperance
movement survived is Sweden, which saw no fighting on its
territory and whose political institutions, including those
of the working class, survived the war relatively unscathed.
Today, the Swedish temperance movement IOGT-NTO has
close to fifty thousand members, many of whom belong to
workers' organizations as well, making it a broad grassroots
movement rooted in popular workers' struggles of the past.

Conclusion
The political problems of Austromarxism seem clear: its
resistance to fascism proved too weak, be it because of wrong
evaluations or because of misplaced restraint and naivety.
Yet the Austromarxist attempt to bridge the gap between
reformist and revolutionary tendencies remains an important challenge for all leftists, and relevant discussions must

continue, regardless of the shortcomings of Austromarxism's political leaders. Furthermore, even if belated, the Austrian workers' movement, largely shaped by the Austromarxists, did not let the fascists simply roll over it.

The positive consequences of the Schutzbund must not be overlooked amidst the frustration over missed opportunities and eventual defeat. The Republican Schutzbund was the first European effort to meet the fascist threat with an armed organization designed specifically for that purpose. It inspired similar organizations in other countries (the German *Reichsbanner Schwarz-Rot-Gold* among them[78]), and Julius Deutsch, as the Schutzbund's chairman, also made efforts to unite all of Europe's antifascist militias in a common body: at a conference in Vienna on July 11, 1926, representatives from Austrian, Belgian, Czechoslovakian, German, Polish, and Yugoslavian workers' militias founded the short-lived *Internationale Kommission zur Abwehr des Faschismus* (International Commission for the Defense Against Fascism).

Even the civil war had some positive outcomes. The common argument that the trauma it caused contributed to the cooperative relationship between the SPÖ and the conservative *Österreichische Volkspartei* (Austrian People's Party, ÖVP) after World War II is of course hardly anything radicals can get excited about; not only did it mean the complete loss of any revolutionary edge among the Social Democrats, but it also created a system of institutional corruption (the infamous Austrian *Proporzsystem*: *Proporz* as in "proportional") that divided up all public posts—from elementary school headmaster to theater director—between the two parties. But indeed encouraging were the impressions the civil war made on antifascists around Europe, and the discussions about antifascist tactics and strategy it caused.[79] Béla Kun, the leader of the 1919 Hungarian Council Republic, wrote a widely distributed 120-page analysis of the events,[80] and

Josef Hindels, one of the few Marxist intellectuals in the SPÖ, summarized the effects as follows: "The Austrian proletariat had suffered defeat. But it was very different from that of the German proletariat in 1933. The Austrian workers' movement was defeated *in battle*; it refused to be enslaved without resistance. Despite the tragic outcome and despite the many victims, the February battle was not without meaning and not in vain. It strengthened antifascist forces around the world and it helped overcome the resignation that Hitler's rise to power had caused in many workers' parties."[81]

With respect to the hesitance of the SDAP and the Schutzbund leaders to engage in battle earlier, Hindels concluded that "any retreat from fascism only makes it stronger and the socialist forces weaker, as they become demoralized and crumble; if we heed this lesson, the heroes of February 1934 did not die for nothing."[82]

The social and cultural achievements of Austromarxism, expressed by "swimming pools for adults, paddling pools for children, dental clinics in schools, and maternity homes"[83] as much as by "adult education centers, lending libraries, bookstores, publishing houses, theaters, and festivals"[84] are also hard to deny. Even Helmut Gruber, author of the fabulous *Red Vienna: Experiment in Working-Class Culture, 1919–1934* and very critical of many of its aspects, draws the following conclusion:

> We ought to remind ourselves that despite serious practical failings, fundamental flaws in conception, and far-reaching dangers, Red Vienna succeeded as no other metropolis had in improvising and innovating social reforms and cultural activities for its working class within the political limits of a polity hostile to such efforts. . . . The Viennese cultural experiment remains the clearest example of the possibilities and limits of providing a foretaste of the socialist utopia in

the present, of devising and implanting a unique proletarian culture in a society that has not experienced
a fundamental revolution.[85]

The problems of the Austromarxists' cultural ambitions—in particular, the "body cultural" ones addressed in
this book—were threefold:

1. *Order and discipline*: The Austromarxist experiment was
   characterized by classical notions of order, discipline,
   and norms that workers had to live up to in order to
   fulfill their historic mission as agents of socialist becoming. The lack of individual freedom and diversity must
   appear as unappealing to most current activists as the
   glorification of (masculine) bodily strength and related
   ideals of beauty and health.

2. *Mass aesthetics and militarization*: Despite the Austromarxists' insistence on embracing antimilitarism,[86]
   military notions strongly characterized their ideas
   about proletarian struggle and the building of socialism,
   while the festivities they organized revealed a fascination for uniform mass performances akin to that of their
   right-wing opponents.

3. *Puritanism and moralism*: It is obvious that the moral
   expectations levied on the Austrian worker by
   Austromarxist leaders rivaled—or exceeded—the
   demands made by religious leaders from their flock.
   Elements of "socialist puritanism"[87] and "paternalism"[88]
   can't be denied, and it seems safe to assume that many
   ordinary workers ignored those expectations.

To reference the context of a bygone era as an explanation for outdated ideas is as legitimate as it is meaning-
less for a contemporary context. Some criticisms of the
Austromarxists must not be overstressed, however. For
example, the "dichotomy between leaders and followers" was
hardly as pronounced as some make it appear.[89] Of course,

ANTIFASCISM, SPORTS, SOBRIETY

there were elitist streaks in the Austromarxists' understanding of socialism and working-class life. Some of their ideals might have also been far removed from real-life aspects of working-class culture. But it is not true that Austromarxism simply was an abstract mind game entertained by bourgeois intellectuals who forced their outlandish ideas on the proletarian rank and file. Julius Deutsch grew up poor in Vienna's working-class quarters.[90] Karl Renner was the eighteenth child of destitute vineyard workers. The SDAP prodigy Joseph Buttinger, later leader of the underground Revolutionary Socialists, was the son of migrant laborers. These are but the most prominent examples of SDAP officials with working-class backgrounds. And the Austromarxist leaders who did not have such a background did at least live up to what they preached. Otto Bauer has been called an "ascetic leader" by former companions.[91]

It also cannot be denied that Austromarxism was a mass movement. The SDAP was voted for by the vast majority of Vienna's working class during the interwar period; hundreds of thousands of workers were members of party-affiliated organizations (whether they dealt with labor issues, sports, or anything "from Esperanto to gardening and philately"[92]); and the print run of some Austromarxist publications—for example Julius Deutsch's *Unter roten Fahnen!*—was a cool three hundred thousand plus. To assume that all of the workers supporting the SDAP, actively participating in its organizations, and reading its literature were duped by elitist leaders is at least as paternalistic as some of the Austromarxists' evaluations of workers' culture might have been.

Notions of order and discipline and a fascination with military-inspired mass aesthetics were—and often still are—characteristic for most revolutionary movements on the Left, safe anarchist ones. This is not the place to rekindle Marxism-vs.-anarchism debates, but much contention revolves around the necessity (or not) of rigid, authoritarian, and uniform mass organizing during the establishment of a socialist society and its defense. While for some Austromarxism might confirm that any Marxist approach will inevitably lead to rigid, authoritarian, and uniform social structures, for others, it might be proof that an armed mass movement cannot be effective without a sense of order, discipline, and cohesion. Be it as it may, the Austromarxist approach provokes debates about popular struggle and movement-building that remain as urgent as ever.

The following texts by Julius Deutsch make much of what has been said more tangible. They attest to a bold and ambitious attempt at bringing the class struggle to everyday life and creating a socialist society. They also attest to wrong analysis, false hopes, and moral harshness. Some readers might find them to confirm the dangers—perhaps even the totalitarian tendencies—implicit in any mass-based movement. Others might appreciate the straightforwardness in moral demands at a time (today) when all "metanarratives" are shunned, which often causes people not to take any stand at all. And others still—perhaps the majority—will find certain parts engaging and others not. In any case, these are documents of an important era in the development of socialist theory and practice, important enough not to be confined to history alone. Revolutionary organizing, the struggle against fascism, and the inclusion of everyday culture into our politics are challenges we are all still facing.

Further Reading

English literature on Austromarxism, Austrian socialism, Red Vienna, and the Austrian Civil War is limited, but some works are outstanding. The two-thousand-page study *Austria: From Habsburg to Hitler* (1980) by Charles A. Gulick provides a broad general overview. Helmut Gruber's *Red Vienna: Experiment in Working-Class Culture, 1919–1934* (1991) introduces the Social Democrats' Vienna specifically. Janek Wasserman's recent *Black Vienna: The Radical Right in the Red City, 1918–1938* (2014) looks at the social democrats' enemies, while Charlie Jeffery's *Social Democracy in the Austrian Provinces 1918–1934: Beyond Red Vienna* (1995) takes a look at the situation in the Austrian countryside.

The demise of the SDAP as well as the February 1934 events are covered in Anson Rabinbach's *The Crisis of Austrian Socialism: From Red Vienna to Civil War, 1927–1934* (1983) and in Ilona Duczynska's *Workers in Arms: The Austrian Schutzbund and the Civil War of 1934* (1978; German original: *Der demokratische Bolschewik. Zur Theorie und Praxis der Gewalt*, 1975); the latter pays particular attention to the organization of the Republican Schutzbund and questions of military strategy. Anson Rabinbach also edited an anthology of historical analyses of the Austromarxist era, namely *The Austrian Socialist Experiment: Social Democracy and Austromarxism, 1918–1934* (1985). Kurt L. Shell's *The Transformation of Austrian Socialism* (1962) is an excellent study on how Austrian Social Democracy changed after World War II.

Texts by Austromarxists in English are found in *Austro-Marxism* (1978), edited by Tom Bottomore and Patrick Goode, and the more recent *Austro-Marxism: The Ideology of Unity* (2015), edited by Mark E. Blum and William Smaldone.

The definitive volume on Austromarxism in German is Norbert Leser's *Zwischen Reformismus und Bolschewismus. Der Austromarxismus als Theorie und Praxis* (Between Reformism and Bolshevism: Austromarxism as Theory and Practice, 1968). In English, the Leser essay "Austro-Marxism: A Reappraisal" was published in *Journal of Contemporary History* (vol. 1, no. 2, April 1966).

The most comprehensive English book on the workers' sport movement is *The Story of Worker Sport* (1996), an anthology edited by Arnd Kruger and James Riordan. The historians Robert F. Wheeler and David A. Steinberg have contributed several articles to academic journals. Among the numerous histories available in German are the classic *Arbeitersport* (Workers' Sport, 1929) by Fritz Wildung and *Illustrierte Geschichte des Arbeitersports* (Illustrated History of Workers' Sport, 1987), edited by Hans Joachim Teichler and Gerhard Hauk.

The standard history of the RSI is *Die Rote Sportinternationale 1921–1937. Kommunistische Massenpolitik im europäischen Arbeitersport* (The Red Sport International 1921–1937: Communist Mass Politics in European Workers' Sport, 2002) by André Gounot. It is not available in English, but several essays by Gounot are, for example "Sports or Political Organization? Structures and Characteristics of the Red Sport International, 1921–1937," in *Journal of Sport History*, vol. 28, no. 1, 2001. Herbert Dierker's book *Arbeitersport im Spannungsfeld der Zwanziger Jahre* (Workers' Sport Amidst the Tensions of the 1920s, 1989) recalls the conflict between the SWSI and the RSI. There are also books in German and French about worker athletes in anti-Nazi resistance groups: *Deutsche Arbeitersportler gegen Faschisten und Militaristen 1929–1933* (German Worker Athletes Against Fascists and Militarists, 1929–1933, 1975) by Günther Wonneberger, *Rote Sportler im antifaschistischen Widerstand* (Red Athletes in the Antifascist Resistance, 1978) by an editorial collective from the former East Germany, and *Les sportifs ouvriers allemande face au nazisme* (German Worker Athletes Against Nazism, 2010) by Guillaume Robin.

For people who enjoy digging in archives, SWSI congress reports (available in various languages, although mostly in German) are well worth exploring. Special treats are the guidebooks of the Workers' Olympics if you can track them down. Film aficionados might enjoy the 1925 documentary film about the Frankfurt Olympics, *Die neue Großmacht* (The

New Great Power), and the 1929 documentary film *Die Frau im Arbeitersport* (Women in Workers' Sport).

★

Unfortunately, few works are available on the historical connections between the workers' movement and the temperance movement. Kate Transchel's excellent *Under the Influence: Working-Class Drinking, Temperance, and Cultural Revolution in Russia, 1895–1932* (2006) traces alcohol policies in the early Soviet Union. *Den skötsamme arbetaren: idéer och ideal i ett norrländskt sågverks-samhälle 1880–1930* (The Orderly Worker: Ideas and Ideals in a Nordic Logging Community, 1880–1930, 1988) by Ronny Ambjörnsson is a great study about the influence of the temperance movement on early Swedish labor organizing.

Notes

1   After the war, Austria—like Germany—was divided into four zones under administrative control of France, Great Britain, the United States, and the Soviet Union, respectively. The capital city, Vienna—like Berlin—was divided accordingly. By 1955, Austrian politicians had negotiated the departure of all Allied powers and their military forces. On May 15 of that year, Austria became independent again.

2   See the article "Was ist Austro-Marxismus?," written by Otto Bauer and published anonymously in *Arbeiter-Zeitung*, November 3, 1927, 1–2. An English translation of the article is included in Tom Bottomore and Patrick Goode, eds., *Austro-Marxism* (Oxford: Clarendon Press, 1978).

3   Renner was also the first chancellor of the Second Republic.

4   See the section "Workers' Militias" for comments on the history of the KPÖ after 1934.

5   Norbert Leser, *Zwischen Reformismus und Bolschewismus. Der Austromarxismus als Theorie und Praxis* (Vienna/Frankfurt/Zurich: Europa, 1968), 298.

6   Quoted from Leopold Spira, "Probleme der österreichischen Arbeiterbewegung nach dem Ersten Weltkrieg," in Arbeitsgemeinschaft für Gewerkschaftliche Einheit und Bewegung für

Sozialismus, ed., *Geschichte der österreichischen Arbeiterbewegung* (Vienna: self-published, 1978), 38.

7   E.J. Hobsbawm, Introduction in Ilona Duczynska, *Workers in Arms: The Austrian Schutzbund and the Civil War of 1934* (New York and London: Monthly Review Press, 1978), 23.

8   Linzer Programm, section 3: "Der Kampf um die Staatsmacht."

9   Karl Radek, "Foundation of the Two and a Half International," *The Communist International*, nos. 16–17 (1922): 31–43.

10 Otto Bauer, *Zwischen zwei Weltkriegen? Die Krise der Weltwirtschaft, der Demokratie und des Sozialismus* (Bratislava: Eugen Prager, 1936), 312.

11 Josef Weidenholzer, "Red Vienna: A New Atlantis?," in Anson Rabinbach, ed., *The Austrian Socialist Experiment: Social Democracy and Austromarxism, 1918–1934* (Boulder and London: Westview, 1985), 198.

12 Anson Rabinbach, Introduction in Rabinbach, ed., *The Austrian Socialist Experiment*, 2.

13 Karl Polanyi, *The Great Transformation* (Boston: Beacon Press, 1957; first edition 1944), 288.

14 Max Adler, *Neue Menschen. Gedanken über sozialistische Erziehung* (Berlin: Laub, 1924).

15 Max Adler in *Der Sozialismus und die Intellektuellen* (1910), here quoted from Bottomore and Goode, eds., *Austro-Marxism*, 262.

16 Julius Deutsch, *Ein weiter Weg* (Vienna: Amalthea, 1960), 38.

17 Ibid., 141.

18 Renamed *Sozialdemokratische Partei Österreichs* in 1991.

19 Ernst Glaser, *Im Umfeld des Austromarxismus. Ein Beitrag zur Geistesgeschichte des österreichischen Sozialismus* (Wien/ München/Zürich: Europaverlag, 1981), 511.

20 Detlev Albers, "Otto Bauer und die Konzeption des 'Integralen Sozialismus'" in D. Albers, J. Hindels, L. Lombardo Radice et al., eds., *Otto Bauer und der "dritte" Weg. Die Wiederentdeckung des Austromarxismus durch Linkssozialisten und Eurokommunisten* (Frankfurt/Main: Campus, 1978), 28–60. For the significance of the Austromarxist enterprise for Gramsci's theory of hegemony, see Helmut Gruber, *Red Vienna: Experiment in Working-Class Culture* (New York and Oxford: Oxford University Press, 1991), 185.

21 "Vorwort," in Albers et al., eds., *Otto Bauer und der "dritte" Weg*, 8.

22 Karl R. Stadler, "Vorwort," in Leser, *Zwischen Reformismus und Bolschewismus*, 14.

23 Leon Trotsky, *My Life* (New York: Charles Scribner's Sons, 1930), 161–64.

24 V.I. Lenin, "Greetings to Italian, French and German Communists (October 10, 1919)," in V.I. Lenin, *Collected Works*, vol. 30 (Moscow: Progress Publishers, 1965), 54.

25 Leser, *Zwischen Reformismus und Bolschewismus*, 502–3.

26 Bauer, *Zwischen zwei Weltkriegen?*, 347.

27 The winning powers of World War I led by Great Britain, France, and Russia.

28 *Arbeiter-Zeitung*, March 23, 1919, 1.

29 See Gabriel Kuhn, ed., *All Power to the Councils! A Documentary History of the German Revolution of 1918–1919* (Oakland: PM Press, 2012).

30 Victor Serge, *Memoirs of a Revolutionary 1901–1941* (London/Oxford/New York: Oxford University Press, 1963; original French edition 1951), 189.

31 Julius Deutsch, *Aus Österreichs Revolution. Militärpolitische Erinnerungen* (Vienna: Wiener Volksbuchhandlung, n.d.), 109.

32 *Kommunistische Internationale* no. 9, March 1920, here quoted from Deutsch, *Aus Österreichs Revolution*, 109.

33 Deutsch, *Aus Österreichs Revolution*, 105.

34 Julius Deutsch, "Der Republikanische Schutzbund," *Der Schutzbund. Monatsschrift des Republikanischen Schutzbundes* no. 1 (June 1924): 1–2.

35 Bauer, *Der Aufstand der österreichischen Arbeiter*, 11. According to Bauer, the Schutzbund was only founded when negotiations by Deutsch with the bourgeois parties about mutual disarmament of the militias had been rejected (ibid., 5).

36 Linzer Programm, section 3: "Der Kampf um die Staatsmacht."

37 Franz West, "Die österreichische Arbeiterbewegung und die Offensive des Faschismus—Vom 15. Juli bis zum 12. Februar 1934," in Arbeitsgemeinschaft für Gewerkschaftliche Einheit und Bewegung für Sozialismus, ed., *Geschichte der österreichischen Arbeiterbewegung*, 47.

38 Norbert Leser, *Der Sturz des Adlers. 120 Jahre österreichische Sozialdemokratie* (Vienna: Kremayr & Scheriau, 2008), 95.

39 Julius Deutsch, "Der 15. Juli," *Der Schutzbund. Monatsschrift des Republikanischen Schutzbundes* no. 9 (September 1927), 129–30.

40 Julius Deutsch, *Antifaschismus. Proletarische Wehrhaftigkeit im Kampfe gegen den Faschismus* (Vienna: Wiener Volksbuchhandlung, 1926), 117. Also: "It is a question of survival for the proletariat to

be neither intimated nor pacified. If it refuses to be thrown to the ground without resistance and to forsake the control of its own destiny, it will at times have no other choice but to take to violence as the last means in the class struggle to defend itself against violent attacks" (ibid., 118).

41 Internationaler Sozialistischer Verband für Arbeitersport und Körperkultur (ISVAK), ed., *Bericht über den IV. Kongress zu Helsingfors, 5.–8. August 1927* (Leipzig: Arbeiter-Turnverlag, n.d.), 57.

42 Bauer, *Der Aufstand der österreichischen Arbeiter*, 24–25. See also Bauer, *Zwischen zwei Weltkriegen?*, 304.

43 Duczynska, *Workers in Arms*, 134. The "odd kind of trinity" refers to a comment by the Prussian general and military theorist Carl von Clausewitz who, in his famed treatise *Vom Kriege* (On War; published posthumously in 1832), called war a *wunderliche Dreifaltigkeit* consisting of (in simplified terms) emotion, chance, and rationality.

44 In Deutsch's defense, he also formulated progressive ideas on warfare in his 1927 book *Wehrmacht und Sozialdemokratie* (Berlin: Dietz, 1927).

45 Duczynska, *Workers in Arms*, 11–12.

46 Ibid., 91.

47 Karl Haas, "Die Wehrpolitik der Sozialdemokratie." Lecture given at the Symposium Austria 1927–1938, October 24, 1972, quoted from Duczynska, *Workers in Arms*, 59.

48 Eduard Ludwig, *Österreichs Sendung im Donauraum* (Vienna: Österreichische Staatsdruckerei, 1954), 221.

49 Deutsch, *Ein weiter Weg*, 207. A longer explanation of the situation in Vienna's inner city during the fighting can be found in Julius Deutsch, *Putsch oder Revolution* (Karlsbad: Graphia, 1934), 40–41.

50 Graz, Austria's second-biggest city where the KPÖ has reached up to 20 percent of the vote in recent municipal elections, remains an exception. See Gabriel Kuhn, "Arnold's Nightmare: The Curious Success of the Communist Party in Graz, Austria," *Counterpunch*, Weekend Edition August 16–18, 2013, counterpunch.org.

51 Duczynska, *Workers in Arms*, 2.

52 Schutzbund member Josef Traschler in Duczynska, *Workers in Arms*, 11.

53 See Julius Deutsch's text "Under Red Flags! From Records to Mass Sport" in this book for more details.

54 Hans Gastgeb, "Panem et circenses," *Der Kampf. Sozialdemokratische Monatsschrift* no. 1 (1933): 38.

55 Robert F. Wheeler, "Organized Sport and Organized Labour: The Workers' Sports Movement," in "Workers' Culture," special issue, *Journal of Contemporary History* 13, no. 2 (1978): 201–2.

56 ISVAK, ed., *Bericht über den IV. Kongress zu Helsingfors*, 57. Twenty years later, Deutsch was even more categorical, stating that "the communists, as advocates of a totalitarian dictatorship, want something categorically different from the parties of democratic socialism" (Julius Deutsch, *Was wollen die Sozialisten?*, Wien: Verlag der Wiener Volksbuchhandlung, 1949, 52).

57 The ASKÖ was refounded after World War II and remains Austria's biggest sports organization to this day. However, it never regained its political significance. In 1971, it characteristically changed its name from *Arbeiterbund* to *Arbeitsgemeinschaft* (while the term *Arbeiterbund*—"workers' league"—was directly linked to the workers' movement, *Arbeitsgemeinschaft*—literally, "working community"—is a generic alternative for "association").

58 The International Labour and Amateur Sports Confederation (*Confédération Sportive Internationale Travailliste et Amateur*, CSIT) was founded in 1946 as a successor to the SWSI but never gained a comparable political profile. In 1986, it was officially recognized by the International Olympic Committee.

59 See Julius Deutsch's text "Under Red Flags! From Records to Mass Sport" in this volume for a more detailed description.

60 ISVAK, ed., *Bericht über den IV. Kongress zu Helsingfors*, 59–60.

61 Deutsch, *Ein weiter Weg*, 93.

62 Cornelius Gellert and Julius Deutsch, "Vorwort," in SASI, ed., *Bericht über den VI. Kongress der Sozialistischen Arbeitersport-internationale in Lüttich am 8., 9. u. 10. September 1932* (Prag: Sozialistische Arbeitersportinternationale, n.d.), 3–4.

63 ISVAK, ed., *Bericht über den IV. Kongress zu Helsingfors*, 57–58.

64 Gruber, *Red Vienna*, 105. Julius Deutsch always objected to the accusation of militarism. See his text "The Organization of Self-Defense" in this book.

65 Leo Tolstoy was a prominent anarchist teetotaler; one of his best-known texts on the question of alcohol, "Why Do Men Stupefy Themselves?" (1890), is available online as a Wikisource. During the Makhnovists' military campaign in the Ukraine, Nestor Makhno issued orders to his troops declaring: "Drunkenness is to be considered a crime. It is a still greater crime for a revolutionary

insurgent to show himself drunk in the street." (Peter Arshinov, *History of the Makhnovist Movement 1918–1921*, London: Freedom Press, 1987 [1923], 219) In the Netherlands, there were close ties between the anarchist movement and the temperance organization *Algemene Nederlandse Geheel-Onthouders Bond* (General Dutch League for Total Sobriety, ANGOB); the annual anarchist Pinksterlanddagen gathering was founded as a sober event in 1927 (this is no longer—or only partly—observed). For Spain, see Burnett Bolloten, *The Spanish Civil War: Revolution and Counterrevolution* (Chapel Hill: University of North Carolina Press, 1991), 68–69. Murray Bookchin explained: "The struggle of the Spanish Anarchists against alcoholism, dissoluteness, and irresponsibility became a struggle for the integrity of the working class, a validation of its moral capacity to reorganize society and manage it on a libertarian basis in an era of material scarcity." (Murray Bookchin, *The Spanish Anarchists* [San Francisco: AK Press, 1998], 51–52). Also in Austria, the most prominent anarchists of the time, Pierre Ramus and Franz Prisching, were sobriety advocates.

66 Ralf Hoffrogge, *Sozialismus und Arbeiterbewegung in Deutschland von den Anfängen bis 1914* (Stuttgart: Schmetterling, 2011), 107.

67 There was stronger resistance to all alcoholic drinks from some libertarian socialists in Germany, such as the editor of the journal *Die Aktion*, Franz Pfemfert.

68 Deutsch, *Ein weiter Weg*, 41.

69 Quoted from Klaus Dede, "Genuß und Mäßigkeit," http://www.ak-trinken.de/galerie/Textsammlung/DAAB-Abstinenten-Bund.html#_ftn37.

70 Quoted from *Der Schutzbund. Monatsschrift des Republikanischen Schutzbundes* no. 8 (August 1925): 6.

71 Deutsch, *Ein weiter Weg*, 12.

72 ISVAK, ed., *Bericht über den IV. Kongress zu Helsingfors*, 33.

73 Carl Schreck, *Arbeitersport und Sozialdemokratie* (Leipzig: Arbeiter-Turn- und -Sportbund, n.d.), 6. Lecture given on May 31, 1929, at the convention of the Social Democratic Party of Germany (*Sozialdemokratische Partei Deutschlands*, SPD) in Magdeburg.

74 Theodor Hartwig, "Körperkultur und Klassenkampf," *Der Schutzbund. Monatsschrift des Republikanischen Schutzbundes* no. 11 (November 1925): 13.

75 Julius Deutsch, "Sportler, meidet den Alkohol!," *Der Weckruf. Zeitschrift des Arbeiter-Abstinentenbundes in der Tschechoslowakischen Republik* no. 3 (June 1936): 1.

76 Leonard Nelson, "Lebensnähe," originally published in the ISK bulletin in 1926, here quoted from Leonard Nelson, *Gesammelte Schriften*, vol. 9 (Hamburg: Meiner, 1972), 374.

77 Even if some radicals might see this as nothing but a welcome shedding of moralistic baggage, it's a sentiment that isn't shared by all analysts of the postwar Left. In his thorough study of the 1970s New Communist Movement, *Revolution in the Air*, Max Elbaum writes:

> There were . . . serious problems with the movement's stance toward alcohol use, which in its early years ranged from complete tolerance to near encouragement on the grounds that drinking was part of working class culture. Whatever the stated policies of a particular group, in practice alcohol abuse was a prevalent (but hardly ever discussed) problem. . . . Problems stemming from substance abuse were found from the base to the top leadership level in several groups. And the dynamics accompanying substance abuse tended to . . . complicate the already serious problem of providing accountability and democracy within their hierarchical structures.

Max Elbaum, *Revolution in the Air: Sixties Radicals Turn to Lenin, Mao and Che* (London/New York: Verso, 2002), 171. Today, it is mainly in anti-colonial and anti-imperialist struggles—ranging from indigenous resistance in North America to Zapatista communities to Third World Maoist armies—that alcohol consumption is raised as a political issue (see, for example, Giibwanisi, "Sobriety: Water Not Fire Water", August 6, 2013, basicnews.ca; Victoria Law with Hilary Klein, "The Untold Story of Women in the Zapatistas," March 13, 2015, bitchmedia.org; Mandira Sharma and Dinesh Prasain, "Gender Dimensions of the People's War: Some Reflections on the Experiences of Rural Women," in: Michael Hutt, ed., *Himalayan "People's War": Nepal's Maoist Rebellion* (London: Hurst & Company, 2004), 152–65.

78 *Reichsbanner Schwarz-Rot-Gold* (The Banner of the Reich: Black, Red, and Gold) was a predominantly social democratic network of antifascist militias founded in 1924.

79 See *Geschichte der Arbeiterbewegung, ITH-Tagungsbericht 9: Arbeiterbewegung und Faschismus. Der Februar 1934 in Österreich*

(Vienna: Europa, 1976). For more international socialist reactions see Gruber, *Red Vienna*, 3–4.

80 The text appeared in 1934 in several languages. The English edition was titled *The February Struggle in Austria and Its Lessons* and published by Workers Library Publishers in New York.

81 Josef Hindels, *Von der ersten Republik zum Zweiten Weltkrieg* (Malmö: Framtiden, 1947), 44.

82 Ibid., 45.

83 Ibid., 33.

84 Rabinbach, Introduction in Rabinbach, ed., *The Austrian Socialist Experiment*, 5.

85 Gruber, *Red Vienna*, 180 and 185.

86 See, for example, Julius Deutsch's text "The Organization of Proletarian Self-Defense" in this book.

87 Kurt L. Shell, *The Transformation of Austrian Socialism* (Albany: State University of New York, 1962), 10.

88 Gruber, *Red Vienna*, 8.

89 Ibid.

90 See "Julius Deutsch: Biographical Notes" in the appendix to this book.

91 Hans Zeisel, "The Austromarxists in 'Red' Vienna: Reflections and Recollections," in Rabinbach, ed., *The Austrian Socialist Experiment*, 122.

92 E.J. Hobsbawm, Introduction in Duczynska, *Workers in Arms*, 19.

PART II

ANTIFASCISM, SPORTS, SOBRIETY

Selected Writings by Julius Deutsch

Julius Deutsch in the 1920s.
(Private collection)

Julius Deutsch

Antifaschismus!

Proletarische Wehrhaftigkeit im Kampfe gegen den Faschismus

Wien 1926

Verlag der Wiener Volksbuchhandlung

(Private collection)

The Organization of Proletarian Self-Defense

Originally published as "Organisation des Selbstschutzes," chapter 3 in *Antifaschismus! Proletarische Wehrhaftigkeit im Kampfe gegen den Faschismus* (Antifascism! Militant Proletarian Defense in the Struggle Against Fascism) (Vienna: Wiener Volksbuchhandlung, 1926).

The traditional aversion of organized workers to militarism makes the creation and the expansion of proletarian defense units difficult. Without the order, discipline, and unity of military divisions, useful defense units cannot be built. There is no particular reason why the proletariat should not use military structures. The problems of militarism are not related to a particular structure. It is not like the sound of military units marching in step hurts the workers' ears. The problem of militarism is related to the army being an element, indeed the most important element, of the power apparatus employed by the state's ruling classes. In this sense, it is clear that organized proletarian self-defense has nothing to do with militarism. It is no machinery of oppression, but, to the contrary, an institution for the defense of working people. Since the purpose of militarism is entirely different, it is also filled with a different spirit (*Geist*), in fact, a nonspirit (*Ungeist*), intentionally alienated from the people in order to serve as an effective means to crush them with neither hesitation nor shame. The inner core of militarism is strange and hostile to the people. The proletarian defense units are entirely different. They belong to the people's flesh and blood. If they were not carried by the people, they would be but pale and lifeless spooks. The purpose and the innermost essence of militarism have nothing in common with the proletarian defense units.

The similarities between the proletarian defense units and the military derive from something very different, namely composition and form. The military teaches us how to mobilize the masses, how to turn them into combat units, and how to lead and guide them. It would be foolish not to use a certain work machine because, under certain circumstances, it can also cause damage. In the same vein, it would be foolish not to use military composition and form because it can cause damage in the hands of the people's enemies. We do not blame the printing press for the production of intellectual poison either.

The division into platoons, companies, and battalions, the chain of command, the movement of military units, these are the things that we have adopted. It is not *militarism*, but *military technique* that is used in proletarian self-defense. Only a critique concerned with superficialities can see a new militarism emerge. It is no surprise, of course, that the enemies of the proletariat conflate proletarian defense with militarism in order to discredit it in the eyes of the workers. But we must not be concerned with the demagogic needs of the enemy. Important is only that the workers are fully and constantly aware of the fundamental difference between militarism and proletarian self-defense.

Parts of military appearance are uniforms and flags as well as the festive colorfulness of military parades. The fascists of all countries have made the most of this. There is no convincing reason why the proletarian defense units should not try to do the same. If uniforms, flags, and marching bands make you appear powerful, then they should be used. People like colors, music, and celebrations, and this must not be disregarded due to misplaced pietism. The clever use of people's emotions must not be left to reactionaries. The enemies of the workers know how to satisfy the masses' needs for spectacle. The organizations of the workers must be at least as impressionable.

We must not underestimate the sense of force and power conveyed by a marching unit. The determined steps of a battalion captivate not only the marching soldiers but also the spectators. Nor must we forget that the proletariat is often accused of unruliness and lack of discipline by its enemies. This is another reason for the significance of a united and orderly proletarian march. It makes the inner power of the movement visible.

The presence of uniformed columns gives the workers' demonstrations a more imposing character. This is not only important for inspiring the participants and for persuading undecided bystanders; it is also important for sending a message to the enemy. The meaning of these demonstrations is to prove that the marching masses can turn into fighting masses if need be. And, indeed, this is how the enemy understands them.

In the countries where proletarian defense units exist, it is crucial to incorporate them into the workers' culture as a whole. They need to be tied to other workers' organizations and occupied in meaningful ways. This is necessary since, in most countries, civil war is latent. It might slumber for a while, but then it breaks out again with full force. The proletarian defense units cannot simply be dissolved during the slumber; as a result, they wouldn't be there when it matters. They must always be ready. Therefore, they must keep themselves busy by supporting other workers' organizations. Without regular activity, they would wither away, like any human organization.

Once we had acknowledged this in Austria, it was not hard to find things to keep the defense units occupied. They began to serve as security during meetings, as campaigners during elections, as strike posts during work stoppages. When there was nothing else to do, they appeared at the festivals of the workers' sport organizations; indeed, they sometimes became the main attraction. One must not underestimate what this entails, even if it might seem insignificant. During festivals, more people come together than on any other occasion. Furthermore, you find many people there who do not join political demonstrations. If the proletarian defense units are involved, they give the festivals special meaning and reach a whole new crowd; people who came for nothing but the spectacle are suddenly filled with a proletarian fighting spirit.

But that is not all. The proletarian defense units fulfill a task within the workers' movement that goes beyond strengthening the fighting spirit and the readiness for self-protection, beyond anything we might consider militant defense (*Wehrhaftigkeit*). That is because their regular routines serve important purposes: they stand for the principle of order; they link the movement's different elements together; they act as the *proletarian militia*. The bigger and broader the units become, the stronger and the more meaningful this role will be. Of course, this in no way diminishes the original purpose of the defense units as a means to combat fascism. And it should not!

One often hears that the proletarian defense units need to be sufficiently armed to fulfill their duty. This is not entirely correct. Of course, the more arms the units have, the bigger their power. But it is not true that the arms are the most important aspect and that no effective defense can be organized without them. The most important aspect is military structure. Without it, effective resistance becomes practically impossible. It is not difficult to get arms in modern countries when they are needed. They can be acquired much faster than useful military units can be formed. This is not to say that proletarian defense units do not require arms or that it is not important to teach their members how to use them. But to simply demand the "arming of the proletariat"—no matter the lack of organization—is inexpedient, and sometimes simply dangerous. Yes, especially at times when the fascists drown in arms, it becomes mandatory for the proletarian defense units to have their own; but the owner is the *organization*, not the individual member. The possession of arms must not be overestimated; it is only overestimated by those who know very little about the complexity of military action.

The experience of all countries where proletarian defense units are active has taught us that their mere presence helps prevent civil war. The enemies of the working class are impressed both by their material power and their self-confidence. Proletarian self-defense is a *means of prevention*. This is its biggest virtue. Wherever the fascists have not yet managed to seize power, wherever they are still engaged in a struggle for the control of the state, their activities have been curtailed by the determined resistance of the proletariat's organized defense forces. If, in certain countries, the fascists have gained the upper hand, it was only because their military techniques were superior. But wherever fascism was confronted not by unorganized individuals but by an organized proletarian defense force, it has failed. Fascist power crumbles whenever it meets organized counterpower. It is not hard to learn the right lesson once we have understood this.

Now let us turn to the structure of the proletarian defense units. It seems easiest to use a concrete example. The Austrian one seems particularly useful: it is the oldest one and the one that has developed the furthest.

The Republican Schutzbund of Austria is a registered society. According to its articles, the society's purpose is the unification of all republican forces in Austria in order to fulfill the following tasks:

1. Protecting the republican constitution.
2. Protecting the members and the property of all organizations representing republican values.

3. Helping the security forces to maintain order and to defend the republic against violent attacks or coups.
4. Providing aid during natural catastrophes.
5. Providing security at the events and demonstrations of republican organizations.

The articles also state that the society is "nonmilitaristic." This is in line with Austrian law, which prohibits the formation of military units. Legally, the Republican Schutzbund is indeed not a military organization. It has military traits, but that does not make it a proper military body. It does not have sufficient arms and no complete military command.

The society is led by a national board. Each Austrian province has a provincial board. Each town has a municipal board. Close relations to other proletarian organizations are strongly encouraged. On all levels, the society's boards include members of the SDAP and trade unions. All actions of the Republican Schutzbund are coordinated with the party leadership. In some cases, party officials directly oversee Schutzbund units.

The Schutzbund units are divided into platoons, companies, and battalions. The chain of command is similar to that of a regular army. Besides conventional units, the Schutzbund also has special task units. The biggest and most important ones are formed by the railway workers and the postal and telegraph workers. There is also a unit formed by municipal gas and electricity workers in Vienna, a bicycle unit, and a well-organized unit of health and sanitation workers, including several doctors. All of the special units are under the national board's command.

The demands that any Schutzbund member (called an *Ordner*, or "marshal") is expected to meet are summarized in the Five Duties printed on each membership card:

Your first duty is *punctuality*! A marshal always has to be on time, whether attending a meeting, an exercise, or an action.

Die fünf Pflichten des Ordners!

Die erste Pflicht ist **Pünktlichkeit!** Der Ordner muß zu jeder Ordneraktion, sei es eine **Versammlung**, eine **Übung** oder ein **Alarm**, genau zur festgesetzten Zeit kommen.

Die zweite Pflicht ist: **Disziplin!** Den Anordnungen der freigewählten Führer ist **unbedingt** Folge zu leisten.

Die dritte Pflicht ist: **Nüchternheit und Verschwiegenheit!** Ein guter Ordner meidet den **Alkohol**; er spricht nicht vor Fremden oder in Wirtshäusern von den Angelegenheiten der Ordnerorganisation.
Während **jeder Aktion** ist der Alkoholgenuß untersagt.

Die vierte Pflicht ist: **Verläßlichkeit!** Der Ordner darf nicht ohne Grund den Versammlungen oder einer Aktion fernbleiben. Kann er nicht kommen, dann muß er den Ordneranschuß rechtzeitig verständigen.

Die fünfte Pflicht ist: **Besonnenheit und Strammheit!** Ruhig und kaltblütig macht der Ordner seinen Dienst. Jeder **geschlossene Aufmarsch** muß schon allein durch seine Strammheit wirken.

Die Zentralleitung.

Wien V, Rechte Wienzeile 97

The Five Duties listed on the back of a Schutzbund membership card. *(Private collection)*

Your second duty is *discipline*! The elected leaders' commands have to be followed under all circumstances.

Your third duty is *sobriety* and *discretion*! A good marshal abstains from alcohol; he does not speak about the organization in front of strangers or in inns. The *consumption of alcohol* is prohibited during any action.

Your fourth duty is *reliability*! A marshal must not miss any meeting or action without excuse. If he cannot participate, he has to notify the board beforehand.

Your fifth duty is *calmness* and *focus*! A marshal carries out his duty with composure, and each public demonstration has to impress by its determination.

Schutzbund members do not receive any monetary compensation for their services. In fact, they pay a small membership fee. In return, they get a subscription to the monthly journal *Der Schutzbund*. In the case of injury during Schutzbund service, they receive support from the Schutzbund fund. Each member has to pay for his own uniform, although other proletarian organizations may provide subsidies for those with no or low income.

A big challenge is the training of the youth. The current members of the Schutzbund are for the most part experienced soldiers who have served in the war. With time, their numbers will dwindle. Who shall take their place? In Austria, we try to solve this with the help of two big proletarian youth networks, the *Verband der jugendlichen Arbeiter* (Association of Young Workers)[1] and the workers' sports clubs. The Association of Young Workers includes training units, in which Schutzbund leaders teach the members all aspects of Schutzbund service. The maximum age for membership in a training unit is eighteen. After that, a member can join the Schutzbund; he has to join by the age of twenty. Usually, an entire unit is transferred from the youth organization to the Schutzbund, so that its members can stay together. The transfer is observed with a public ceremony, which includes marches, speeches, music, and a pledge of allegiance to the Schutzbund flag.

The young men in the workers' sports clubs are prepared for the Schutzbund in a similar way. The only difference is that the sports clubs' units do not have to be transferred to the Schutzbund. They can remain in the clubs, where they form special units (*Wehrturnerzüge*: Gymnasts' Militant Defense Platoons). These units are administered by the sports clubs but ready to serve the Schutzbund at any time. The reason for the units remaining in the sports clubs is that they can practice *Wehrturnen* (Militant Defense Gymnastics). Wehrturnen includes combat exercises of all sorts, not only gymnastics. It might also be connected to other forms of combat training. The Schutzbund probably benefits less from the physical training in the Wehrturnerzüge than from the strong fighting spirit that is nurtured there.

In order to instill this spirit in the Austrian proletariat as early as possible, the education starts with the youngest. In the proletarian children's organization *Kinderfreunde* (Friends of the Children), special groups have been formed

Early Red Falcons parade. *(Kinderfreunde Österreich)*

under the name *Rote Falken* (Red Falcons).[2] The Red Falcons engage in numerous communal activities and are modeled after scouting groups. They are motivated by youthful romanticism and want their members to be wild and brave, like actual falcons. They engage in fights and value loyalty. The difference to the bourgeois and nationalist scouts is that for the Red Falcons loyalty means loyalty to the working class. The Red Falcons' twelve commandments are the following:

1. A Red Falcon pledges allegiance to the working class.
2. A Red Falcon is always loyal to his comrades.
3. A Red Falcon sees every workingman as his friend and brother.
4. A Red Falcon is always ready to help others.
5. A Red Falcon respects honesty and conviction, even among his enemies.
6. A Red Falcon follows the orders of an elected leader.
7. A Red Falcon is courageous and never gives up.
8. A Red Falcon is truthful; you can trust his word; he is reliable and punctual.

JULIUS DEUTSCH

9. A Red Falcon's thoughts, words, and deeds are always pure.
10. A Red Falcon abstains from and fights all intoxicants.
11. A Red Falcon looks after his body and exercises.
12. A Red Falcon is a friend and protector of nature.

Such a program suits the dreams and wishes of fine boys well. The Red Falcons wear a uniform, of course, even if it is a simple one. There is a direct path from the Red Falcons to the *Ordner der Jugendlichen* (Youth Marshals),[3] to the Wehrturnerzüge, and then on to the Schutzbund. The more youth it attracts, the stronger the roots of the proletarian defense units will be. The Austrian beginnings have been very promising. With the rise of antifascist self-defense units across Europe, their effects will soon extend far beyond the country's borders.

Notes

1   The *Verband jugendlicher Arbeiter* was founded in 1902; it was renamed *Sozialistische Arbeiter-Jugend* (Socialist Workers' Youth, SAJ) in 1919. Deutsch uses a variation of the original name. The SAJ's successor, the *Sozialistische Jugend Österreich* (Socialist Youth Austria, SJÖ), was founded in 1946 and exists to this day. All notes by Gabriel Kuhn.

2   The organization *Kinderfreunde* was founded in 1908 and integrated into the SDAP in 1921. The first Red Falcon groups, bringing together children aged twelve to fifteen, were formed in 1925. Both Friends of the Children and Red Falcons exist to this day.

3   This was probably a short-lived youth chapter of the Schutzbund; I was not able to find any records.

Alkoholkapitalismus

Illustration from *Der abstinente Arbeiter. Organ des Deutschen Arbeiter-Abstinenten-Bundes*, March 15, 1926. (*Private collection*)

WIENER
SOZIALDEMOKRATISCHE
BÜCHEREI

Unter roten Fahnen!

Vom Rekord- zum Massensport

Von Julius Deutsch

WIEN 1931
VERLAG DER ORGANISATION WIEN
DER SOZIALDEMOKRATISCHEN PARTEI

(Private collection)

Under Red Flags! From Records to Mass Sports

Originally published as *Unter roten Fahnen! Vom Rekord- zum Massensport* (Vienna: Organisation Wien der Sozialdemokratischen Partei, 1931) and issued as a pamphlet ahead of the 1931 Workers' Olympics in Vienna. The text is an updated and abbreviated version of the book *Sport und Politik* (Sport and Politics, 1928).

Older people—and they don't have to be very old—will remember how the worker spent his Sundays twenty or thirty years ago. After the week's hardships, the most important thing was to sleep in. Then he got ready for a lunch that wasn't necessarily sufficient, but a step up from the usual fare. A short nap followed, and then he headed to the inn. There he sat comfortably at the beer table until the evening— or longer, depending on how far his hard-earned money got him.

Of course, not all workers spent their Sundays that way, but there were hundreds of thousands who did not know of any other pleasure, and who did not want to do anything other than spend their only day off in a stupor. If you consider that the average working time in the factories was nine and a half to ten hours per day, and in some smaller workshops eleven hours or more, this is no surprise. The workers simply got so worn out by a week of drudgery that they could not think of anything but a Sunday on which they did nothing; nothing at all.

The proletarian youth did not elevate themselves above the superficial pleasures of imitating the bourgeoisie either. As the saying goes, "The young ones chirp as the old ones sing."[1] When the father went to the inn, the son did not want to miss out. The only difference was that the younger generation might have headed for a café instead of a tavern. But in both cases the Sunday pleasure consisted of sitting around in smoky premises, playing cards, and drinking alcohol.

It is true that, at times, the youth's interest in sports took them away from this dull and uninspiring milieu. But their interest in sports mainly consisted of marveling at the performances of extraordinary athletes. In particular, the big soccer arenas drew thousands of young proletarians. There they got terribly excited about one star player or the other and ecstatic when one of their idols left the arena as a winner.

If proletarian boys and girls practiced sports themselves, they belonged to clubs controlled by the bourgeoisie. Without realizing it, they adopted the ideas and thoughts of the propertied classes. They never noticed that these allegedly "neutral" clubs were not neutral at all. Of course, one didn't talk much about politics. Club officials carefully avoided upsetting the young workers. Yet, the social dynamics of the bourgeois sports clubs were destined to alienate the worker from his own class. He got preoccupied with all sorts of things that had nothing to do with his economic interests. Step by step, he was absorbed by the superficiality and emptiness of bourgeois life, until it no longer mattered that he was not being taken seriously and only tolerated as an outsider. With time, all healthy proletarian caution disappeared and the young athlete no longer had any interest in the ambitions of his class; instead, he comfortably settled into the world of "neutral" sport.

There were not only "neutral" sports clubs and associations, of course, but also those that served the interests of the propertied classes openly. These clubs were undisguised fighting units of the bourgeois youth, sailing under national- ist, and sometimes religious, flags.

For a long time, the nationalist parties of Austria did not have any sports associations of their own; they were all asso- ciated with the German ones. To this day, these associations form the backbone of the nationalist movement. Once upon a time, they mostly propagated pan-German ideas; today, they fill the ranks of the National Socialists.

Regardless of whether the bourgeois sports clubs and associations try to appear neutral or admit to their politi- cal aims, they inevitably practice sports in a way adapted to capitalist thinking and feeling. In sport as in economic life, the success of the individual is everything. A world of sport dominated by the propertied classes is individualis- tic; it cannot be any other way.[2] In capitalism, success is the only thing that matters. Everyone tries to make it to the top in order to acquire money and fame. All means are accept- able, because once you are at the top, no one cares about how crooked or straight the path was that got you there.

The brutal and egotistical desire for success that char- acterizes capitalism is reflected in bourgeois sport. Here, too, the individual attempts to rise to the top without any consid- eration for others; here, too, we find the desire for money and fame outweighing everything else.

In order to measure individual success, records are required. In bourgeois sport, setting new records becomes the ultimate goal. In fact, bourgeois sport has degenerated into a mad obsession with records. When a ski jumper jumps seventy meters, the next one will not rest until he jumps seventy-five meters, which will inevitably prompt a third to do everything in his power to jump even further. It is a spiral with no end but broken bones. And ski jumping is but one example. We see the same in running, long jumping and high jumping, pot shooting, weightlifting, swimming, and all other disciplines. Exaggerated high-end performances are the essence of bourgeois sport.

We must not be misunderstood: of course we are not in principle against high-end performances. We are not against athletes measuring their abilities in noble competition and trying to improve their achievements. But we are strictly against sports turning into the hypertrophy of singular muscles. Sports should develop all parts of the body harmoniously. We are against sports as an assembly of artistic stunts that replace balanced exercise with the disproportionate focus on a single ability. Artistic stunts belong to the circus, and people who enjoy watching them can go there. But no one will convince us that they have anything to do with sports, especially since we need to consider that it is nearly impossible to achieve such specialization for anyone with a regular job. The focus on high-end performances leads inevitably from amateur to professional sport.

That said, we have nothing against professional sport as such. The profession of an athlete is as honorable as any other. But sport as a profession has nothing to do with sport as a means to strengthen the people. We are happy for any professional athlete earning a decent income and we hope for him to increase it. But we are against reducing sport to professional sport because our vision is not that of a few professional athletes mesmerizing the world with stunning feats; our vision is that of hundreds of thousands—indeed, millions—of people becoming healthier and stronger thanks to training.

It is inevitable that the obsession with records and the commercial exploitation that characterize bourgeois sport attract sensationalism, advertising, low instincts, and unsavory businesses. We only need to look at the big events of bourgeois sport to find this confirmed. For weeks, the advertisement machines are rolling at full steam, until finally tens of thousands of people gather at the day of reckoning. With all the passion that has been artificially whipped up they watch some record hunters compete for a big prize. The prize is as much part of the commercial ballyhoo as all the rest of it. The rawer and the more dangerous the sport, the bigger the attraction. Boxing matches trump all others. When Tunney and Dempsey fought in Chicago for the world title, the bourgeois sports associations and journals hyped the event for weeks, getting the public ready for the big battle. Then, when the highly anticipated day finally arrived, an audience of 160,000 people reacted like madmen to each swing and hook thrown by one of the opponents. The entire world followed the bloody spectacle in front of the radio. Some people got so excited, they suffered a stroke. These sad consequences did not interfere with the event's success, of course. Why would a few dead fans matter when everyone is marveling at the money earned by the boxing champs: one million dollars here, half a million dollars there? And this doesn't include all the money that was made from advertisements, ticket sales, and bets. Yes, this was indeed a historic day for bourgeois sport.[3]

It is true, even some representatives of bourgeois sports associations criticized this particular event. But it is not true that this particular event was a mere distortion of bourgeois sport. This is a sorry excuse and a hypercritical cover-up. The Chicago boxing match represented the essence of bourgeois sport. Look at other bourgeois sports events: aren't they characterized by all the same traits, only in the Chicago case they were gigantically grotesque?

All that bourgeois sport focuses on is individual performance. It is about records, records, and more records. *Records* is the magic word that everything revolves around. It appears as if there is no bigger excitement in life than watching a high jumper clear 1.90 meters instead of 1.85. The running achievements of a Nurmi or a Dr. Pelzer are hailed as quasi miracles and reproduced without end in sensationalist media reports. The same is true for the swimming achievements of a Johnny Weißmüller or an Arne Borg, as well as the different attempts to cross the English Channel, the Gibraltar Strait, or some other stretch of water. But the human being is no amphibian and should not have the ambition to become one either. For the development of humanity it is completely irrelevant whether Fräulein Eberle manages to cross the English Channel or not. Likewise, it does not belong to the great moments of human evolution when, in America, a Mr. Charles Hofmann manages to beat the record for aileron rolls by turning his plane around its own axis 1,093 times.[4] One "master athlete" claims a record in dancing, a second in climbing trees, a third in flying an airplane for weeks on end, and a fourth in hopping from Vienna to Paris on one leg. . . . Wonderful! But our aims are different. We do not want to breed master athletes and chase records. We want to strengthen the people.

In this respect, we have seen a development of enormous cultural and historic proportions during the last decade. As soon as the factory bells announce the end of the workday, the proletarian youth rush out the door and head for sports grounds. As long as there is no thunderstorm, the grounds are busy every day. We see all sorts of sports being played. Even sports that once were the exclusive domain of the propertied classes have been taken over by the proletariat. Today we can rightfully say that there is no sport left in which the youth of the propertied classes outdoes the proletarian youth.

The precondition for the sports activities of the masses is the reduction of working hours. As long as workers had to toil ten, eleven, or even more hours per day, it was impossible to engage in any ambitious sports program. It was the eight-hour workday that gave rise to workers' sport. This was not the only factor, of course. All of the social achievements since the end of the war form the basis on which workers' sport has developed. Mass sport is a living testimony to the rise of the working class. The healthy and strong bodies of the worker athletes are proof that a new kind of human being is forming whose ideals differ from those of previous generations.

Workers' sport differs at its very core from the sport of the propertied classes. While the latter is *individualistic*, the former is *collectivist*. While bourgeois sport champions *individual performance and records*, workers' sport champions *mass achievements and solidarity*.

The terms *bourgeois sport* and *workers' sport* do not only indicate political opposites. They also indicate deep *factual differences*. Their very essence is different. Workers' sport is closely tied to the development of a new *proletarian culture*. It has made enormous contributions to the workers leaving the inns and going hiking in beautiful landscapes instead; it has taught them to develop all parts of their bodies and to prevent injuries; it has provided them with courage and self-confidence and strengthened the belief in their own power, thereby also creating the necessary conditions for intellectual development.[5] Rather than an innocent pleasure far from intellectual relevance, workers' sport is a means to elevate the working masses from a dull and quasi-bourgeois existence to the radiating heights of a new culture.

It is no coincidence that, of all workers' sport organizations, the *Naturfreunde* (Friends of Nature) have left the deepest mark on the proletariat. An ethical organization through and through, it was founded in Vienna in 1895. It soon expanded and has conquered all of the countries where independent workers' movements exist. Today, the Friends of Nature have turned into an international hiking association of extraordinary dimensions. The organization owns 420 cottages and hostels in the world's most beautiful sceneries. Its symbol—a brotherly handshake—flies on flags in Europe, America, and Australia.

★

Each of the big workers' sport events attests to the cultural ambitions of the worker athletes. The events are not only a demonstration of the athletes' goals—socialism, peace, and fraternity between peoples—but their structure also signifies a conscious break with the past and a desire to create a new culture.

Recently, German Member of Parliament Cornelius Gellert related an anecdote in the Reichstag[6] that reveals the spirit separating the worker athlete from other young people: When, in July 1929, the German worker athletes held their great sports festival in Nuremberg, the Dürer House, which hosts the works of the immortal master Albrecht Dürer, had no less than 13,300 visitors. When some weeks later, on August 14, the National Socialists gathered in Nuremberg for a big demonstration, not even one hundred of them deemed it necessary to honor the representative of a culture they are supposedly so proud of.

We can find confirmations for these differences everywhere. While working-class youth relish cultural achievements, the National Socialists hardly recognize the achievements of their own people despite their glorious nationalistic propaganda. Part of the modern working class's desire to form a new culture as an expression of its own proper will is making the culture that exists its own.

The ultimate goal is to form the future of humankind anew. This will require huge and passionate struggles, and workers' sport makes an important contribution to them by providing the strong and determined fighters that are needed. *Workers' sport strengthens the working masses.* It is in this very sense that workers' sport has an immediate impact on the course of history, which is characterized by the confrontation between capitalism and socialism. In this confrontation, which marks our time, the youth cannot be passive. By preparing the young workers for it, workers' sport forges the tools of a new world.

Workers' sport is directly linked to the modern working class's ambition for culture and freedom. For a long time, this link has not been recognized and the contributions of the worker athletes have been underestimated even within the social democratic parties. As long as the parties and the affiliated unions were small and weak, all forces available had to be put to their use. Any organization developing apart from these two pillars of the proletarian movement was seen as a distraction rather than an aid. Today, this has changed. After having existed merely alongside each other for some time, workers' sport and the overall workers' movement have now found each other and feel they belong together. Paul Franken has made this very clear in his preface to Wildung's well-known book.[7] He writes: "The workers' movement has broadened since the war and the new conditions have caused high ambitions in proletarian cultural independence. The worker athletes' efforts concerning the culture of the body are an essential part of the proletariat's cultural efforts in general." He continues:

> The values of the old world are deeply etched into the hearts and minds of the working people. This is where the great transformation must begin, and it must begin with a socialist education of character and perception. This is not only a question of political power, but also of the spiritual and moral qualities of the people who want to build a new world. To educate and form these people is the (very difficult) task of socialist cultural efforts, which cannot be strictly separated from other efforts of the modern workers' movement. *All branches of the modern workers' movement depend on one another and inspire one another.* If some "only politicians" still consider their activities the only ones of importance it is a remnant of days long gone.

★

During the last years, the conflict between labor and capital has intensified. Fearing to lose power once and for all, the propertied classes have resorted to means of violence. In Italy, Hungary, Yugoslavia, Romania, Lithuania, and Poland they have managed to use the state for enforcing their violent rule over the working class. The rule of the people, democracy, has been strangled in these countries. Instead, bloody and ruthless dictatorships gag the working masses.

In other countries, the propertied classes try to do the same. Fierce struggles engulf Germany. And even in countries with old and strongly rooted democracies, such as France, Belgium, England, and the Scandinavian states, fascist ideologies make headway within the bourgeoisie.

In Austria, we have had to repel a wave of fascist attacks over the past two years. We were facing a reactionary onslaught with strong financial backing and ruthless methods. Hard and exhausting struggles lie behind us. It has not been easy to hold out against the storm.

Now that the weapons are resting, it is time to reflect on what has happened and to draw the necessary conclusions for the next round. There cannot be any doubt that a next round will come. Our enemies are already preparing for it, and they are threatening us. It may be that the form of the confrontation will be different, as will the composition of the enemy's lines; for example, the Heimwehr militiamen might be replaced by National Socialists. But we will not be spared the struggle itself. That is why reflecting upon what has happened is crucial. We need to be prepared for what is about to come.

The recent struggles were struggles of the youth. Militias stood on both sides. Naturally, they were mainly formed by young people. Next to the militias, the sports organizations were of huge importance, again, on both sides. Let us consider the particularly revealing role of the German and Austrian Alpine Club as an example.[8] Under the pretense of keeping Jews away, the Alpine Club denied all workers access to its cottages. It has used its monopoly on the Alpine terrain to make it impossible for people with undesirable ideas to even visit there. But that is far from all. The Alpine Club has also turned into a formidable meeting place for all reactionary elements opposed to the rise of the working class. And the Alpine Club really is but one example. Other sports organizations of the propertied classes are filled with the same hatred. This is particularly true for the biggest among them: on September 25, 1927, the *Bundeswehrturnauschuß des Deutschen Turnerbundes 1919* (Committee for Military Affairs of the German Gymnastics Association 1919, BWTA[9]), to which most gymnastics clubs of the bourgeoisie belong, sent a newsletter to all of their affiliated bodies. It contained the following revealing paragraphs:

> We have come to an agreement with the national board of Austria's alpine self-defense organizations, according to which it is the duty of the SS units and the *Heimatwehren*[10] to arm the militant units of the German Gymnastics Association if necessary.
>
> The BWTA does not consider this a satisfying solution to the question of armament, however, since the weapons might be delivered too late. In general, it is desirable that our militant units can act as independently as possible. Since neither the gymnastics association's national board nor any of its affiliates on the regional and municipal level have the means to purchase weapons and other equipment, we recommend to the militant units to raise funds among active and supporting members as well as among friendly organizations, businesses, and corporations. It is up to the individual unit to decide whether to be frank about the usage of the funds or whether to claim them for some

other activity. In numerous places, *Heimatwehren* have already had very successful fundraising campaigns.

Relevant equipment is all of the following: rifles, sword knots, machine guns, ammunition, shovels, pots, field kitchens, tarps, first aid kits, shoulder bags, and backpacks. All equipment should be as uniform as possible.

This newsletter discloses beyond a doubt that our country's national gymnastics clubs are filled with a fascist spirit. Four years ago, they had already approached company owners (!) for money to acquire weapons in preparation for civil war. Since then, their fascist convictions have become even stronger. The Turnerbund 1919 is on the best way to become the main fighting force of the National Socialists.

In the March 1, 1931, issue of the *Bundesturnzeitung* (National Gymnastics Journal), the "Wehrturner" supplement opened with a call from the BTWA and the national board of the German Gymnastics Association. The call included the following line: "Our association must be a *völkisch* fighting unit and spread its ideas among wide parts of the population."[11] The national board subsequently demanded: "We have to be tenacious and tireless in our educational and organizational efforts to prepare each gymnast for militant action, that is, to train all members (within the realms of possibility) in ways enabling them to serve the people *with weapons in hand*. To be a gymnast means to be ready to fight. In the future, there shall not be a distinction between a gymnast and a militant gymnast."

It is clear that the militancy referenced here has nothing to do with defending the country against exterior enemies. No, the militancy of the German gymnast is directed against the "enemy within," that is, social democracy. The gymnastics clubs have turned into fascist fighting units waiting for the right moment to attack.

Under these circumstances, the working class has no choice but to prepare its defense. Our sports organizations must be ready; they must be determined and prepared to defend democracy and the rights of the working people. This is why we have introduced a new discipline to our sports organizations: *Wehrsport*.[12] It intends to train young workers in the means of defense, that is, it teaches them to move in closed formations, to endure long marches, to overcome obstacles, to handle firearms, and to engage in other forms of fighting.

The Helsinki congress of the Socialist Workers' Sport International[13] has clarified Wehrsport's moral principles. They focus on the need for defense; they clearly reject *any intention of attack*. The minutes from the congress state:

> The necessary struggle against fascism does not intend to establish socialism by means of violence. The working class prepares itself for the use of violence only as a *last resort*. In light of the coming final confrontation between the classes, this preparation is necessary.
>
> The workers of Austria, Latvia, Germany, and Belgium have already created defense organizations. With the rise of the fascist movement in other countries, the working classes there will be forced to do the same. As organizations responsible for the physical strength of the proletariat, it is the duty of the workers' sports associations of all countries to support these proletarian defense units by all means possible.

Wehrsport will be performed during the Vienna Olympics. For the first time, representatives of the proletarian defense units will perform alongside worker athletes to demonstrate the means available for improving the working class's fighting power.

★

Sport has not only gained importance in the political struggle between the classes in recent years. It has also begun to play an important part in the economic struggle. In many towns, company owners have enrolled their workers in company sports clubs. These claim to be completely neutral; apparently, they serve no other purpose but to keep the company workers occupied after working hours in the most innocent manner. The companies often provide the sports grounds and the equipment for free or at very low cost. Even financial aid is involved here and there. This, of course, is all portrayed as an act of selflessness.

In reality, the only purpose of company sports clubs is to influence and, in the end, control the workers. The athletes are kept dependent on the companies and therefore compliant. Furthermore, the workers are systematically alienated from their class interests, as they enter an environment that abounds with false pretensions of the supposed harmony between labor and capital. The ultimate goal is to cut the cord between the workers and their political and economic organizations.

There are not only company sports clubs. Also the government and its institutions have founded sports clubs for their employees. There are police sports clubs, postal sports clubs, railway sports clubs, etc. They all have the same innocent claims: they serve a social purpose and create unity; they bring together the upper and the lower classes to play sports together, nothing else. As if by accident, it is of course always the upper classes that control these clubs. How unfortunate!

The true intentions are all too obvious: they are to alienate the worker athletes from their class-conscious peers. We can see the effects already among the proletarian youth. Independent union organizing is suffering both in companies (which have also founded their own apprentice sports clubs) and in government offices.

Without doing them injustice, most company sports clubs can be called *yellow* clubs.[14] The free unions have recognized this and taken countermeasures by forming union sports clubs. These have established themselves relatively quickly and already play an important part in the workers' sport movement. In Vienna, especially, they have been met with enthusiasm.

The bourgeois parties of our country make life difficult for the workers' sport organizations whenever they can. In the towns under their control, there are no gymnasiums or sports grounds available to worker athletes. Although workers' sport organizations are highly dependent on public subsidies since their members are anything but wealthy, they receive no or very little funding. In contrast, the bourgeois parties use all the tricks to secure a wide range of advantages for their own sports clubs. This rule applies to all levels of government, from national to provincial to municipal.

Let us look at the national government's budget as an example. In the year 1931, a total of 280,500 schillings was allocated for the support of sports, but only five thousand of those went to the ASKÖ. This means that the government spends almost sixty times more money on bourgeois sport than on workers' sport, although the organizations of the latter have more members. And the expenses for the physical education of high school and university students—which, essentially, function as hidden subsidies for bourgeois sport—are not even included here. The shamelessness of bourgeois class rule couldn't be more obvious.

Social Democrats have drawn their conclusions from this and try as much as they can to support workers' sport with municipal means. In Vienna and other towns administered by them, they attempt to create an infrastructure serving workers' sport as well as others. The Vienna Stadium, one of Europe's most beautiful sports arenas, is a shining example.[15] Yet we must admit that the building of sports facilities has not kept pace with the blistering development of workers' sport. Many more sports grounds are needed to satisfy the existing needs to at least some degree.

Aware of this, the SDAP passed a resolution at their last party convention in Vienna in 1930, which called on all Social Democratic delegates at the national, provincial, and municipal levels to campaign in their constituencies and legislatures for the support of the workers' sport movement. Most importantly, they were requested to secure regular budget allocations to physical education and workers' sport by the state, the provinces, and the municipalities. Hopefully, these wishes will become a reality! In any case, we can be assured of the good will of the Social Democratic delegates; there is no lack thereof.

No sector of the proletarian movement has striven for international organization faster and more dedicatedly than workers' sport. As soon as worker athletes had overcome the difficulties of establishing organizations in their home countries, they went on to organize on an international level. In fact, the urge for international organization lies in the nature of sport. Also bourgeois sport organizes beyond national borders and arranges international competitions. Yet, it always encounters problems, since its members are strongly attached to national identities. The international events of bourgeois sport suffer from the highly developed chauvinism of the propertied classes; often enough, they even become new sources of national hatred rather than an aid in fostering international understanding.

The international events of workers' sport are different. They serve true fraternity between peoples. They come from the heart and they touch the heart. Each of them serves the ideal of international understanding and peace.

Even before the war, when the workers' sport movement was still weak and undeveloped, attempts were made to unite it internationally. In 1913, the representatives of workers' sports associations from different countries met in Ghent, Belgium. At first, their intention was only to arrange international competitions. But it soon became apparent that they had more in common than mere practical interests. Their ideas went far beyond the arrangement of athletic events. Based on this, the first Socialist Workers' Sport International was founded.

When the war started, the first SWSI dissolved in the same way that all international organizations of the proletariat dissolved. After the end of the war, however, it made a comeback. In 1920, worker athletes met again, this time in Lucerne, Switzerland, under the chairmanship of the Belgian Gaston Bridoux. At the meeting, the program was formulated that would guide the organization's work during the following years. Its most important sections read as follows:

> The International Workers' Association for Sports and Body Culture[16] consists of national associations for physical education, gymnastics, sports, and hiking. Its goal is to propagate physical training, sports, gymnastics, and hiking among the working class, especially among the youth of both genders. *Physical education is as essential for the international proletariat as its moral advance.* The workers' sport movement is no less important than the workers' political, union, and cooperative movements. The fight against capitalism, nationalism, and militarism must also take place in sports.
>
> Based on the maxim that a healthy mind can only live in a healthy body, our organization intends to

put all aspects of physical health, especially physical training, *in the service of the proletariat*; physically and mentally, the proletariat needs to become as strong as possible. But in a capitalist society, this goal can never be fully achieved, since the capitalist mode of production grants the proletariat neither the time nor the resources for the best physical training. In other words, our ambitions can only be realized in a socialist society. Therefore, we only accept members who share this vision. . . .

We demand from the socialist parties and trade unions of all countries that they do their utter best to help our organization reach its goals as soon as possible. These goals reflect an existential interest of the proletariat. We also urge all socialist parties and trade unions to see to it that none of their members join bourgeois sports clubs and associations. The bourgeois sports associations have always been among the strongest supporters of nationalism and chauvinism. They have aroused the youth's passion for militarism and bear significant responsibility for the catastrophe that has devastated Europe and killed its best sons.

We direct the following call to the worker athletes everywhere: "Unite! Dispersed you are nothing, but united you are a power that can shake the world!"

The words of this manifesto were heard around the globe. The echo it found in most European countries was louder than ever expected. In 1913, when representatives of national workers' sport organizations held their first international meeting, they counted about 220,000 members between them. This number had risen to 1,500,000 at the time of the Helsinki congress in 1927. Two years later, when the delegates met in Prague, there were already 1,700,000 registered worker athletes. And at the time of the Vienna

Olympics, the membership of the Socialist Workers' Sport International is likely to exceed the proud number of two million.

Membership has risen in almost all European countries. In Germany, Austria, and Czechoslovakia, where there already was an independent workers' sport movement before the war, the growth after the war has been tremendous. Soon, there were hundreds of thousands of worker athletes in these countries. Also in France, Belgium, and Switzerland the development has been positive. Recently, workers' sport has even gained a foothold in the homeland of sports, England. The movement has also expanded to the Netherlands and the Scandinavian countries. In Scandinavia, Denmark was the entry point, but Norway now has the most developed workers' sport culture. Only Sweden remains on the outside, but things will change there, too.[17] Meanwhile, developments have been excellent in Finland. The country took the lead in northeastern Europe and keeps it to this day. Latvia and Estonia are following. In the Latvian republic, a truly splendid workers' sport movement has emerged, both in quantity and quality.[18]

Unsurprisingly, the development has been less encouraging in the countries ruled—entirely or partly—by fascists. But with the exception of Italy, where any attempt at founding workers' sports associations was literally drowned in blood, there are signs of hope everywhere. The relatively strongest workers' sports associations in these countries exist in Hungary and Poland, but they have also been established in Romania and Yugoslavia.

Finally, it must be noted that the idea of independent workers' sport has expanded beyond Europe. In America, the movement is growing slowly but steadily. There are also workers' sport organizations in Palestine. At the next World Olympics of Workers' Sport, held in Vienna in late July 1931, worker athletes from all these countries will participate. The

Arbeiterolympiade:
Official symbol of
the 1931 Worker's
Olympics in Vienna.
(Private collection)

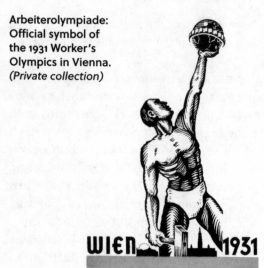

event will be the biggest sports demonstration the world has ever seen. But not only are the exterior dimensions of the Olympics impressive. Even more impressive is the spirit with which they are filled.

During the Olympics, the passion for independent workers' sport, cultural ambition, the strengthening of the proletarian masses, international fraternity, peace, and socialism will find a worthy expression. Under red flags, worker athletes from all over the world will march past the delegates of the International Socialist Congress, which will assemble in Vienna at the same time. This is a symbolic act of deep meaning. Proletarian youth strengthened by sports will unite with the militants of the socialist parties for a global demonstration of the noble goals pursued by the peoples on their way to freedom and peace.

Notes

1   *Wie die Alten sungen, so zwitscherten die Jungen* is an old German saying. "Like father, like son" is a close English equivalent. All notes in this text by Gabriel Kuhn.

2   In *Sport und Politik*, Deutsch writes: "The recklessness and rawness, which we can often witness on sports grounds, are typical characteristics of bourgeois sport, while workers' sport hardly knows of them" (Berlin: Dietz, 1928, 35). While this is certainly a biased assessment, the spirit of fair play that permeated workers' sport has been widely documented; see, for example, Rolf Frommhagen, *Die andere Fussball-Nationalmannschaft. Bundesauwahl der deutschen Arbeitersportler 1924–1932* (Göttingen: Die Werkstatt, 2011).

3   The paragraph refers to the so-called "Long Count Fight" for the world heavyweight title between Gene Tunney and Jack Dempsey. The fight took place in Chicago on September 22, 1927. At the time, it was the biggest commercial sporting event ever.

4   Paavo Nurmi from Finland and Otto Peltzer from Germany were among the world's best middle- and long-distance runners of the 1920s. The American Johnny Weißmüller (Weissmuller), famous for portraying Tarzan in Hollywood movies during the 1930s and '40s, and the Swede Arne Borg were successful swimmers. On August 6, 1927, the American Gertrude Eberle was the first woman ever to swim across the English Channel. The identity of Charles Hofmann could not be verified.

5   In *Sport und Politik* (Berlin: Dietz, 1928), Deutsch elaborates on this point:

> Everyone will become healthier and therefore happier by practicing sports. For those most oppressed in the current economic system, however, it is also a source of liberation. When workers break the chains of monotonous labor deforming their bodies and find themselves on the sports ground, the human being in them awakens, which the capitalist mode of production had stunted. When the workingwoman throws off her garbs and exercises in much more comfortable sportswear, not only her beauty increases but with it her joy for life, which has been suffocated by a ridiculously prude morality. The people who, as the main victims of the present order, have had to suffer the most are those who have the most to win by free athletic activity. (17–18)

Deutsch adds: "The young workers who, through athletic activity, have made their bodies smoother and stronger gain *self-confidence*. For them, controlling the body means to liberate themselves from feelings of inferiority, which they can easily give in to otherwise" (41).

6   1. Cornelius Gellert was a German Social Democrat active in the workers' sport movement; he assisted Julius Deutsch in the SWSI administration. 2. Reichstag was the name for the German parliament used until 1945. The building where the current parliament convenes is still called Reichstagsgebäude, "Reichstag building."

7   Fritz Wildung's Der Arbeitersport (Berlin: Bücherkreis, 1929) is a classic account of workers' sport. See "Further Reading" in Part 1 of this book.

8   In 1873, the Austrian Alpine Club (Österreichischer Alpenverein, founded in 1862) and the German Alpine Club (Deutscher Alpenverein, founded in 1869) merged. Since 1945, they have been administered independently.

9   The Deutscher Turnerbund 1919 was founded in September 1919 as an association of mainly Austrian gymnastics clubs. The attribute German was commonly used in Austria during the interwar period; the country was also commonly referred to as German Austria (Deutschösterreich), although the name had been prohibited by the winning powers of World War I.

10   A rarely used term for the Austrian Heimwehr units.

11   The völkisch movement (völkisch literally means "of the people") was a predominantly reactionary early twentieth-century popular movement in Germany that focused on the cultural and racial unity of a people, also in connection to its particular natural surroundings. It was in many ways an ideological forerunner to National Socialism.

12   See also pages 31–33.

13   The SWSI convened in Helsinki in 1927; see also pages 31–32.

14   The color yellow was associated with conservative politics in the First Austrian Republic, since the flag of the old Austrian Empire was yellow and black.

15   The Vienna Stadium was inaugurated for the Vienna Workers' Olympics of 1931. It was one of the most modern stadiums in Europe at the time and officially called Praterstadion due to its location in the Prater park (best known for its pleasure grounds). Today, it carries the name Ernst Happel Stadium and remains Austria's main sports arena.

16   This was an alternate name for SWSI.

17   This might seem ironic given the strength of the Swedish Social Democrats who gained power in 1920. However, their vision of

the *folkhem* (people's home) was based on a social compromise and any form of class antagonism eyed skeptically. Workers were encouraged to organize in "people's" organizations rather than in "proletarian" ones, and workers' sport never flourished outside of small communist circles.

18 Official membership numbers per country published by the SWSI in 1931 were as follows: America 697; Austria 293,700; Belgium 12,909; Czechoslovakia 207,703; Denmark 20,000; Estonia 1,600; Finland 30,257; France 10,859; Germany 1,211,468; Great Britain 5,000; Hungary 1,750; Latvia 5,171; the Netherlands 16,795; Palestine 4,250; Poland 14,222; Romania 2,500; Switzerland 21,624; Yugoslavia 1,800 (SASI, ed., *Bericht vom VI. Kongressder Sozialistischen Arbeitersportinternationale in Lüttich*, addendum).

Dr. Julius Deutsch

Klassenkampf Disziplin und Alkohol

Wien 1924

Verlag: Buchhandlung des Arbeiter-Abstinentenbundes in
Oesterreich, Wien, VII., Seidengasse 17.

(Private collection)

Class Struggle, Discipline, and Alcohol

Originally published as a pamphlet under the title *Klassenkampf, Disziplin und Alkohol* (Vienna: Buchhandlung des Arbeiter-Abstinentenbundes, 1924); the text is based on a talk given at the general assembly of the *Arbeiter-Abstinentenbund* (AAB) on November 25, 1923.

Class struggle! The mere expression sends shivers down the spines of the bourgeoisie. Whenever the average intellectual encounters it, he leaps into a passionate speech—with all the pathos reserved for festive occasions—propagating the people's unity above all class divisions. But neither the fear of the bourgeoisie nor the empty words of the intellectual can change reality. Reality is determined by economic conditions. The question is not whether we *wish* for a class struggle. The class struggle simply exists. It is a *fact*, and we have to accept it as such, just like the wind and the weather.

Social democracy has two major duties. First, it has to make the working class understand that class struggle is everywhere. Second, it must—and this is the crucial part—teach the working class *how to be victorious* in the class struggle in order to abolish all classes and to establish a classless socialist society.

The proletariat's class struggle is necessarily a mass struggle. For this struggle to be successful, iron discipline is mandatory. Now, some of you might ask: what does discipline have to do with alcohol? This is the question I will try to answer here.

Communal life demands order. If everyone does as he pleases, and if no one shows any consideration for the next man, then eventually everyone will have to suffer and any sense of community will be replaced by the fight of all against all. *There is no community without order!*

What is true for human communities in general is particularly true for the *fighting associations of the people*. They not only demand the general order required by any community, but the submission of the individual will under the communal will. This is, in all brevity, what we understand by discipline.

Of course, our proletarian associations are not coercive. They rest on the principle of voluntary association. This is why proletarian discipline cannot be ensured in the same way that discipline can be ensured in coercive organizations. For example, in the military no one is interested in the will of the individual soldier. The soldier is obliged to obey, and this obligation is enforced by the threat of severe punishment. Such methods are neither possible nor desirable in a political organization. Hence, the discipline in our ranks can and must not rest on coercion, but it has to rest on the voluntary submission of the individual will to the communal will.

How do we reach voluntary discipline? How do we strengthen the proletarian struggle, which we cannot win unless such discipline is established? There is only one way: the fighting proletarians have to develop certain *personal qualities*. It is a big mistake to believe that any working class, no matter its moral and intellectual level, is able to realize socialism. In order to fight successfully, we need people who are indeed *able to fight*.

Now, first and foremost, we are talking about the *physical ability* to fight. Proletarians still work and live under conditions that are detrimental to their health. The heavy labor, the stuffed workplaces, the bad—at times even poisonous—air they breathe all impact their health. Add to this cramped living quarters, insufficient food supplies, poor hygiene, and chronic diseases. Is it surprising that the physical force of the worker leaves a lot to be desired?

Science teaches us that the consumption of alcohol has a negative impact on the body, even the healthiest one. How much more negative must the impact be on the body of the worker, weakened by hardship and misery? Of course, the alcohol lobby has a good press (it can afford it), which speaks of beer as "liquid bread" and wine as "salubrious tonic." But these are all lies. Beer, wine, and liquor are sources of neither nutrition nor strength. They are dangerous means of deception. While providing an imaginary boost, they are, in fact, weakening the body's power of resistance. This is why we advise workers to abstain from alcohol. It doesn't help them; it *damages* them. How much proletarian health has been left behind in inns and on ale-benches!

Away from the inn! Away from sitting around in unhealthy environments! This is a call for heading out into the beautiful countryside, a call for true recreation and recovering.

However, the proletarian liberation struggle needs more than physical strength. Most important, indeed, is the workers' *mental* strength. The workers must understand the conditions of their existence and the possibilities of the working class's advancement. Without *intellectual clarity* and *iron will* the rise of the proletariat is not possible.

Intellectual clarity requires that the workers overcome traditional prejudices, that they overcome their poor, one-dimensional education, and that they—through a profound investigation of themselves—come to see the world as it really is and not as their class enemies make it appear to be.

Nothing makes intellectual clarity more difficult than alcohol. It obscures the brain; it makes it dull and hollow. Anyone involved in political action has experienced this hundreds of times: backwardness and alcohol, stupidity and drowsiness are intrinsically linked; one begets the other. Wherever the alcoholic plague cannot be contained, the best of the socialist prophets speak in vain. Those preoccupied with beer and wine will not understand them. Only when the alcoholic haze is lifted will free and clear thoughts be able to enter the mind. Overcoming alcohol is a requirement for the awakening and maturing of the working class.

The realization of the necessity of the liberation struggle must be accompanied by the *iron will* to engage in it. Is there anything that suffocates this will more than alcohol? Is there anything that makes you more phlegmatic than the beer table of the philistine? Is there anything causing more confusion than boozy mindlessness? The working class must not suffocate its will, become phlegmatic, and let its attentiveness be drowned in blessed dizziness. This is why we fight alcohol: it is *one of the biggest obstacles to the proletarian liberation struggle*.

A fighting working class is like a big army. It must not only reflect the general order mentioned above, but also the strict submission of the individual will to the communal will. Without this, no army can fight. But since we neither have nor want any means of coercion in order to enforce the discipline necessary, it must come from each individual's own free will. It suffices to think of drunk men—fully drunk, half drunk, or even a quarter drunk—to understand that they will never muster this. The first obstacle is the following: people used to drinking are not used to thinking. This is commonly summarized by the saying: "Drinking workers don't think, thinking workers don't drink." Those who are slaves to alcohol will hardly be the free, clear-thinking people that our movement needs. The second obstacle is that alcohol interferes with the normal functions of our brain. Proletarian struggle demands healthy and clear minds. Alcohol must not get in the way. A third obstacle is drinking habits. They take an awful lot of a workingman's time, and they place him in a superficial and quasi-bourgeois environment that paralyzes any proletarian fighting spirit. There has not been a single debate in the party or in the union that wasn't poisoned by comrades gossiping in inns. Whenever gossip causes disarray within the party, we can be certain that it emerged from loose tongues around a beer table. To chatter about party affairs in an inn is not only a nuisance, it also undermines party discipline, which is necessary for the growth of the workers' movement as a whole.

Some among us have drawn the following conclusion: alcohol is a private matter. But is that true? I don't think so. In my opinion, alcoholism is not an individual matter but a social one. Drink not only harms the individual; it harms society. In fact, particularly so. Within the workers' movement—and there especially—the breaches of discipline connected to drink are not a matter that concerns the drinker alone, but something that concerns all of us; our efforts for the party and the union are threatened by the lack of discipline of drinking workers. This is why we decidedly reject the notion that alcoholism is a private matter that we not need to address. We want to state loud and clear that alcohol is an *important social matter*, in particular with respect to working-class struggle.

Let us provide a few examples. Think of the struggles of the unions. They demand prudence and a proper understanding of current power balances. Now, a few glasses of beer or wine are enough for a worker to feel very courageous, in fact, *overly* courageous. Of course, once the effects of the "spirits" are gone, the fighting "spirit" is gone, too. But then it is too late! Important decisions, decisions of *great significance for all of us*, have already been made under the influence of alcohol, giving a very false image of the true mood and will of the proletariat.

If alcohol is a big problem for making proper decisions, it is an equally big problem for the *implementation* of decisions. In our struggle, the implementation of decisions demands courage, endurance, and perseverance. Each election, each propaganda campaign, each strike, each demonstration demands plenty of work and personal dedication of the individual comrade. We can say without exaggeration that the success of almost any serious activity depends on whether the comrades taking it on are—and stay!—sober.

It is telling that in the workers' organization that demands the highest personal commitment and willingness to make sacrifices, sobriety has become accepted as a necessity almost by itself. The organization I am speaking of is the Republican Schutzbund. Very early on, it became clear to the organization's leaders that the success of any action depended to a large degree on whether the membership was sober or not. Today, even Schutzbund members who are not teetotalers make sure that none of the organization's activities are endangered by the consumption of alcohol. The effectiveness of the organization is to a significant degree dependent on sobriety.

As I have already suggested, not all Schutzbund members are teetotalers. In fact, teetotalers don't even make up a significant part of the membership. But the dangers related to alcohol are so obvious that everyone avoids it when on duty. In my opinion, the special challenges faced by Schutzbund members only anticipate the challenges that will one day be faced by all proletarian organizations: the abandonment of the old drinking habits.

Discipline and alcohol are incompatible. If you want one of the two, you can't have the other. Since our organization simply cannot exist without discipline, we have to turn against alcohol.

Proletarian discipline is not slavish obedience to certain exterior things; it is a part of our *ethos*. We are loyal to one another, we practice solidarity, and we obey the resolutions of our representatives because the power of our movement and the possibility of success depend on it. In short, *discipline and solidarity belong together*! To keep discipline means to practice solidarity and to contribute significantly to the working class's advancement. Discipline and solidarity are expressions of proletarian ethics. In this regard, alcohol is not only an enemy of the proletariat in general, but also a specific danger for its inner moral force. This is why we repeat: *those who are serious about expanding proletarian organizations and about the intellectual and moral power of the working class cannot escape the fight against alcohol!*

Finally, let us turn our attention to the significance of the fight against alcohol in the proletarian youth movement. It has almost become a given that there is no drinking at the events of the Friends of the Children and the Youth Marshals.[1] This is one of the biggest future hopes for our class. If our youth grows up without alcohol, the socialist movement will earn new, unimagined sources of power.

The working class must learn to use its own power and to rely on nothing else. Alcohol distorts the difficulties we are facing, and it distorts our own strength. However, we need committed action informed by clear vision; we need the power of solidarity based on discipline. This is why—with the interest of the future and the development of the proletarian organizations in mind—we raise the rallying cry: *Away with alcohol!*

Notes

1   For information on these organizations, see Julius Deutsch's text "The Organization of Proletarian Self-Defense" in this book.

Julius Deutsch:
Biographical Notes

Julius Deutsch was born in 1884 in the village of Lackenbach, Burgenland, today the easternmost province of Austria. His father worked as an innkeeper. Julius was one of four children. When Julius was in kindergarten, the family moved to Vienna, where his father tried to find better-paid work, but things did not go as hoped. The Deutschs lived in poor working-class quarters, with Julius's father struggling to find steady employment. To make matters worse, he had an accident while working as a horsecar driver. Health insurance or disability pensions for workers were almost unheard of in Austria at the time, and, in Julius Deutsch's words, his father "became an invalid hardly thirty-five years old."[1] Shortly thereafter, Julius's mother died of what Julius called the "proletarian disease," tuberculosis.[2]

At the age of fourteen, Julius began an apprenticeship as a printer. He also started to frequent socialist meetings, trade union halls, and workers' education centers. His activities caught the attention of Victor Adler,[3] the figurehead of Austrian socialism and the SDAP chairman. After Deutsch had abandoned his apprenticeship ("I got tired of being but an errand boy"[4]) and spent a couple of years as a migrant worker in western Austria and southern Germany, Victor Adler ensured that he got a high school diploma allowing him to pursue university studies. Adler advised Deutsch to do so away from Vienna not to get distracted by too much political work. Therefore, from 1905 to 1908, Deutsch studied national economy in Zurich, Paris, and Berlin. In Berlin, he met some of the most prominent socialist figures of the era such as Rosa Luxemburg, Karl Kautsky, and August Bebel. Still a student, Deutsch got married to Josefine Schall, whom he had met at a temperance movement event in Vienna. They had a son together, Gustav.[5]

Upon finishing his studies, Deutsch returned to Vienna, began climbing the ranks of the SDAP, and moved closer to the inner Austromarxist circle. About the legendary meetings at Café Central—also attended regularly by Leon Trotsky during his 1907–1914 residence in Vienna—Deutsch wrote the following: "I was invited to them and I was happy to join. But I listened more than I talked. In order to talk much in this circle one needed gifts I didn't possess. I was used to thinking about complicated things until they could be reduced to a simple formula. . . . Opposite masters of discourse like Trotsky, Otto Bauer, and Max Adler it was hard for me to stand my ground."[6]

Deutsch excelled in other aspects. He soon became one of the most respected party organizers with a particular talent for diplomacy. Ilona Duczynska ascribed to him "a gift for impressing and activating people in personal encounters."[7] He was also a skillful analyst and writer focusing on empirical and historical studies.[8]

Deutsch's party career was interrupted in 1914, when he was drafted into the Imperial and Royal Army of the Austro-Hungarian Empire at the outbreak of World War I. Despite his opposition to the war, he served his duty, but not without establishing an illegal network of insurgent soldiers, which, according to the historian Norbert Leser, "was a very risky endeavor that could have easily led to a conviction for high treason."[9] The network remained undetected, however, and the dissolution of the Austro-Hungarian Empire in November 1918 with the subsequent proclamation of the

Austrian Republic meant that Deutsch and his associates were safe.

The first government of the Austrian Republic was a coalition of three parties led by the Social Democrat Karl Renner. Based on his military experience, Deutsch was appointed minister for defense. While Deutsch was active in many parts of the workers' movement and occupied numerous posts, his military credentials would always remain at the center of his political life. In 1923, they made him chairman of the Republican Schutzbund and, in 1936, a military adviser in the Spanish Civil War, when Deutsch offered his services to the republican government after Franco's troops had started their attack. This ended two years of exile in Czechoslovakia where Deutsch had escaped to after the Austrian Civil War of February 1934.

After the fall of the Spanish Republic in 1939, Deutsch left for France, where he escaped encampment—a fate met by thousands of international volunteers—due to his prominent status in the European socialist community. Deutsch lobbied against the encampment system, at one time suggesting integration of the antifascist fighters into the French Army, but to little avail. In Paris, he became the president of *Concentration*, an association of German and Austrian socialists, and the editor of *Krieg und Frieden* (War and Peace), an international journal on military and political issues that appeared for two seasons.

When German troops entered France and descended on Paris in the summer of 1940, Deutsch was offered asylum in the Dominican Republic, probably because exiled veterans from the Spanish Civil War had pushed the agenda. Under adventurous circumstances, he traveled by boat to Cuba, where he was detained with hundreds of other refugees. Deutsch described the months he spent in the country as an endless struggle with bureaucracy and bribery.[10] In addition, he got a bad impression of the dictatorship of General

Rafael Trujillo in the nearby Dominican Republic. Therefore, he applied for a visa to move to the United States, which was eventually granted.

In late 1940, Deutsch arrived in Florida and soon relocated to New York, where he got involved with various initiatives, among them the Austrian Labor Committee and the aid organization Associated Austrian Relief.[11] Deutsch also wrote radio messages to the Austrian people that were broadcasted by the U.S. Office of War Information. During this time, Deutsch met the writer Hertha Strack, another Austrian refugee better known under the pen name Adrienne Thomas. Strack would stay by Deutsch's side until the end of his life. Deutsch's first wife, Josefine, died in 1942. When the war ended in 1945, Deutsch was one of the first Austrian refugees to return home.

Julius Deutsch never occupied a prominent post in the SPÖ. In his memoirs, he claimed that he did not want to stand in the way of social democratic renewal, but it is quite likely that the party officials wanted to keep him at a distance anyway. Austromarxism seemed discredited, and the new leaders clearly veered toward a strictly moderate and reformist line.[12] In 1962, the historian Kurt L. Shell passed the following judgment on the SPÖ: "though the Austrian Socialist Party of today proudly proclaims its identity with its historical predecessors, no visible trace of the former radicalism in thought or temper remains. No other socialist party has traveled a longer road faster from Left to Right."[13]

Norbert Leser summed up Deutsch's role for the SPÖ thus: "As the highest ranking from the old party who returned, he functioned as a living bridge, a personified connection and reference point between old and new."[14] Deutsch also influenced the SPÖ party platform with his 1949 booklet *Was wollen die Sozialisten?* (What Do the Socialists Want?), joined party delegations on foreign visits due to his high international profile, and was influential in shaping Austria's postwar neutrality. He also got work as the chairman of the socialist publishing and distribution house *Konzentration*.

Still, Deutsch was increasingly deemed an Austromarxist burden by the reformist and pragmatic SPÖ leadership. In 1950, he resigned from his post at *Konzentration* amidst internal disputes. Two years later, he testified as a witness—truthfully—in a trial concerning a party financing scandal, shedding bad light on the party leadership. As a result, the leaders tried to expel Deutsch. Although Deutsch still had too many supporters among the rank and file to let this happen, he became a persona non grata among the top tier. This would not change until his death, which caused him much bitterness.

However, it did not stop him from engaging in public debate. On January 17, 1968, he spoke about his life at an adult education center—an Austrian remnant of the old workers' education centers—in the Vienna district of Brigittenau. He collapsed halfway through his speech and died on the way to the hospital. An end as tragic as fitting for a lifetime of socialist agitation.

Julius Deutsch, the Jew

Along with other prominent Austromarxists, most importantly Victor Adler (who converted to Protestantism in 1878) and Otto Bauer, as well as many leading intellectual and cultural figures of Red Vienna, Julius Deutsch was born into a Jewish family. Like many other socialists, he was also an agnostic, downplaying any religious, cultural, and ethnic affiliation. In his case, this went as far as not mentioning his Jewish identity once in the 460 pages of his memoirs. In a 2008 article in the journal *Das Jüdische Echo* (The Jewish Echo), the Austrian political scientist Anton Pelinka commented on this peculiarity thus: "Julius Deutsch was no religious Jew. He took the freedom to abandon his Jewishness. Yet the fact that he never wrote about this decision only

JULIUS DEUTSCH

shows how problematic the relationship to his Jewish identity must have been."[15]

Deutsch represents one of the tragic aspects of belonging to a historically discriminated community. There was no escaping anti-Semitism. Deutsch, Bauer, and other prominent SDAP figures of Jewish descent were constantly subjected to anti-Semitic abuse by their political opponents, and there was widespread anti-Semitism within the SDAP itself.[16] As Anton Pelinka points out, it was fair and sound for Deutsch to present himself as a political refugee rather than a Jew, but had he fallen into the hands of the Nazis, no such distinction would have been made: he would have been classified as a Jew and treated as such—that is, even worse than as a political prisoner.

Analyzing Deutsch's Jewishness and the way he dealt with it would deserve a study of its own. It would not only tell us more about Julius Deutsch but also about the history of Jewish identity and, not least, the connections between Judaism and Austrian culture, which includes Austrian social democracy. In a 2008 volume dedicated to Otto Bauer and Austromarxism, the editors wrote in their preface: "The fact that the mediation between the workers' movement and modernity was guided to a large degree by Jewish intellectuals—both men and women—must not only be mentioned for the sake of historical accuracy, but also because it explains why Austrian social democracy could not, and did not want to, reconnect to its legacy after 1945."[17]

Notes

1 Deutsch, Ein weiter Weg, 26.
2 Ibid., 15.
3 Sometimes spelled Viktor.
4 Deutsch, Ein weiter Weg, 33.
5 For more about Gustav Deutsch, in particular his fate in the Soviet Union, see pages 24–25.
6 Deutsch, Ein weiter Weg, 90.

7   Duczynska, *Workers in Arms*, 30.

8   See Julius Deutsch's bibliography in the appendix of this book for a selection of the most important titles.

9   Leser, *Zwischen Reformismus und Bolschewismus*, 294.

10 Deutsch, *Ein weiter Weg*, 346–57.

11 The Austrian Labor Committee was founded by Friedrich Adler—who also was in exile in the U.S.—in 1942. It was a successor to AVOES (see page 25), which was disbanded the same year. Until the end of the war, the Austrian Labor Committee functioned as the internationally recognized foreign representation of Austrian socialists.

12 Ironically, the name change from *Sozialdemokratisch* to *Sozialistisch* would suggest otherwise, but this was mainly a gesture to appease the Revolutionary Socialists, the most active Austrian socialist group during the war. However, the influence of the Revolutionary Socialists on the SPÖ soon waned. In 1991, the SPÖ finally abandoned the epithet *socialist*, changing its name to *Sozialdemokratische Partei Österreichs*.

13 Shell, *The Transformation of Austrian Socialism*, 4.

14 Leser, *Der Sturz des Adlers*, 134.

15 Anton Pelinka, "Mainstreaming der jüdischen Identität," *Das Jüdische Echo* 57 (November 2008): 120.

16 Jack Jacobs, "Austrian Social Democracy and the Jewish Question in the First Republic," in Rabinbach, *The Austrian Socialist Experiment*, 157–68.

17 Peter Fleissner, Lisbeth N. Trallori, and Walter Baier, "Vorwort: Austromarxismus und die Reform der Revolution," in Walter Baier, Lisbeth N. Trallori, Derek Weber, eds., *Otto Bauer und der Austromarxismus. 'Integraler Sozialismus' und die heutige Linke* (Berlin: Karl Dietz Verlag, 2008), 12.

Julius Deutsch:
Selected Bibliography

From 1903 to 1960, Julius Deutsch authored over thirty books and pamphlets on a wide range of topics, including the Austrian workers' and union movement, military questions, fascism and antifascism, sports, and the Austrian Civil War. The following is a selection of his most important works.

Die Lehrlingsfrage (1903)
"The Apprentice Question." The first pamphlet written by Julius Deutsch, analyzing the situation of apprentices in Austria and demanding an improvement of their rights. Deutsch would publish various pamphlets and booklets on labor-related issues before World War I, for example *Die Tarifverträge in Österreich* (Collective Bargaining Agreements in Austria, 1908), and on early nationalist attempts to infiltrate the workers' movement, for example *Dokumente der Schande. Beweise für den Verrat der deutschnationalen Arbeiterpartei* (Documents of Shame: Proof for the Betrayal by the German National Workers' Party, 1910), which addressed the situation in Sudetenland, the formerly German-speaking territories in the modern-day Czech Republic.

Die Kinderarbeit und ihre Bekämpfung (1907)
"Child Labor and the Fight Against It." Deutsch's first book, investigating child labor in Switzerland and Germany. The

publication followed Deutsch winning the first price in an essay competition on child labor at the University of Zurich.

Geschichte der österreichischen Gewerkschaftsbewegung (1908) "History of the Austrian Trade Union Movement." The first-ever book on the subject.

Das moderne Proletariat. Eine sozialpsychologische Studie (with Rudolf Broda, 1910) "The Modern Proletariat: A Socio-Psychological Investigation." An extensive comparative study of the working classes in several countries. Rudolf Broda was a sociologist friend of Deutsch who taught at universities in France and the United States. French edition as *Le prolétariat international* (1912).

Geschichte der deutschösterreichischen Arbeiterbewegung (1919) "History of the German-Austrian Workers' Movement." Concise history of the workers' movement in the German-speaking part of the Austro-Hungarian Empire. Subsequent editions in 1922 and 1947.

Aus Österreichs Revolution (1921) "From Austria's Revolution." Deutsch's account of the end of World War I and the collapse of the Austro-Hungarian Empire.

Antifaschismus! Proletarische Wehrhaftigkeit im Kampfe gegen den Faschismus (1926) "Antifascism! Militant Proletarian Defense in the Struggle Against Fascism." Book-length analysis of the fascist threat looming over Europe in the 1920s. Deutsch had published similar texts in previous years, among them *Die Faschistengefahr* (The Fascist Threat, 1923), *Wer rüstet zum Bürgerkrieg? Neue Beweise für die Rüstungen der Reaktion* (Who Is Preparing for Civil War? New Proof for the Armament of the Reactionary Forces, 1923), and *Schwarzgelbe Verschwörer*

(Black and Yellow Conspirators, 1925; black and yellow were the colors of the flag of the old Austrian Empire). In 1929, Deutsch's *Der Faschismus in Europa. Eine Übersicht* (Fascism in Europe: An Overview) was published. An English translation of chapter 3 from *Antifaschismus! Proletarische Wehrhaftigkeit im Kampfe gegen den Faschismus*, "Organisation des Selbstschutzes," is included in this book.

Sport und Politik (1928)
"Sport and Politics." Commissioned by the Socialist Workers' Sport International, the book summarizes Deutsch's understanding of workers' sport and includes a history of the Socialist Workers' Sport International. An updated and abbreviated version appeared ahead of the 1931 Workers' Olympics in Vienna as *Unter roten Fahnen! Vom Rekord- zum Massensport*. An English translation of the latter is included in this book.

Der Bürgerkrieg in Österreich. Eine Darstellung von Mitkämpfern und Augenzeugen (1934)
Documentary volume on the Austrian Civil War, translated into Czech, Dutch, English, Norwegian, and Swedish. English edition: *The Civil War in Austria: A First-Hand Account from Eye-Witnesses and Participants* (Chicago: The Socialist Party, 1934).

Putsch oder Revolution? Randbemerkungen über Strategie und Taktik im Bürgerkrieg (1934)
"Coup or Revolution? Marginalia on Strategy and Tactics in Civil War." Analytical study of the civil war in Austria, interlaced with general reflections on armed struggle and revolution.

Was wollen die Sozialisten? (1949)
"What Do the Socialists Want?" Deutsch's socialist vision post–World War II. The book influenced the first party platform of the newly founded SPÖ.

Wesen und Wandlung der Diktaturen (1953)
"The Nature and Transformations of Dictatorships." Deutsch's reflections on totalitarian regimes, mainly in twentieth-century Europe.

Ein weiter Weg (1960)
"A Long Way." Deutsch's memoirs.

ABOUT PM PRESS

PM Press was founded at the end of 2007
by a small collection of folks with decades of
publishing, media, and organizing experience.
PM Press co-conspirators have published and
distributed hundreds of books, pamphlets,
CDs, and DVDs. Members of PM have
founded enduring book fairs, spearheaded victorious tenant organizing
campaigns, and worked closely with bookstores, academic conferences,
and even rock bands to deliver political and challenging ideas to all walks
of life. We're old enough to know what we're doing and young enough to
know what's at stake.

We seek to create radical and stimulating fiction and non-fiction books,
pamphlets, T-shirts, visual and audio materials to entertain, educate,
and inspire you. We aim to distribute these through every available
channel with every available technology—whether that means you are
seeing anarchist classics at our bookfair stalls, reading our latest vegan
cookbook at the café, downloading geeky fiction e-books, or digging new
music and timely videos from our website.

PM Press is always on the lookout for talented and skilled volunteers,
artists, activists, and writers to work with. If you have a great idea for a
project or can contribute in some way, please get in touch.

PM Press
PO Box 23912
Oakland, CA 94623
www.pmpress.org

FRIENDS OF PM PRESS

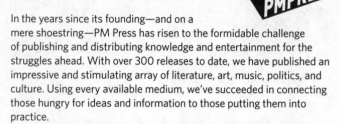

These are indisputably momentous times—the financial system is melting down globally and the Empire is stumbling. Now more than ever there is a vital need for radical ideas.

In the years since its founding—and on a mere shoestring—PM Press has risen to the formidable challenge of publishing and distributing knowledge and entertainment for the struggles ahead. With over 300 releases to date, we have published an impressive and stimulating array of literature, art, music, politics, and culture. Using every available medium, we've succeeded in connecting those hungry for ideas and information to those putting them into practice.

Friends of PM allows you to directly help impact, amplify, and revitalize the discourse and actions of radical writers, filmmakers, and artists. It provides us with a stable foundation from which we can build upon our early successes and provides a much-needed subsidy for the materials that can't necessarily pay their own way. You can help make that happen—and receive every new title automatically delivered to your door once a month—by joining as a Friend of PM Press. And, we'll throw in a free T-shirt when you sign up.

Here are your options:

• **$30 a month** Get all books and pamphlets plus 50% discount on all webstore purchases

• **$40 a month** Get all PM Press releases (including CDs and DVDs) plus 50% discount on all webstore purchases

• **$100 a month** Superstar—Everything plus PM merchandise, free downloads, and 50% discount on all webstore purchases

For those who can't afford $30 or more a month, we're introducing **Sustainer Rates** at $15, $10 and $5. Sustainers get a free PM Press T-shirt and a 50% discount on all purchases from our website.

Your Visa or Mastercard will be billed once a month, until you tell us to stop. Or until our efforts succeed in bringing the revolution around. Or the financial meltdown of Capital makes plastic redundant. Whichever comes first.

Playing as if the World Mattered: An Illustrated History of Activism in Sports

Gabriel Kuhn

ISBN: 978-1-62963-097-7
$14.95   160 pages

The world of sports is often associated with commercialism, corruption, and reckless competition. Liberals have objected to sport being used for political propaganda, and leftists have decried its role in distracting the masses from the class struggle. Yet, since the beginning of organized sports, athletes, fans, and officials have tried to administer and play it in ways that strengthen, rather than hinder, progressive social change. From the workers' sports movement in the early twentieth century to the civil rights struggle transforming sports in the 1960s to the current global network of grassroots sports clubs, there has been a growing desire to include sports in the struggle for liberation and social justice. It is a struggle that has produced larger-than-life figures like Muhammad Ali and iconic images such as the Black Power salute by Tommie Smith and John Carlos at the 1968 Mexico Olympics. It is also a struggle that has seen sport fans in increasing number reclaiming the games they love from undemocratic associations, greedy owners, and corporate interests.

With the help of over a hundred full-color illustrations—from posters and leaflets to paintings and photographs—*Playing as if the World Mattered* makes this history tangible. Extensive lists of resources, including publications, films, and websites, will allow the reader to explore areas of interest further.

Being the first illustrated history of its kind, *Playing as if the World Mattered* introduces an understanding of sports beyond chauvinistic jingoism, corporate media chat rooms, and multi-billion-dollar business deals.

"*Gabriel Kuhn dismantles the myth that sports and politics do not belong together.*"
—Mats Runvall, *Yelah*

"*Creativity and solidarity are as indispensable in sport as they are in social struggle. If you have any doubt, read this book.*"
—Wally Rosell, editor of *Éloge de la passe: changer le sport pour changer le monde*

All Power to the Councils!: A Documentary History of the German Revolution of 1918-1919

Edited and translated by
Gabriel Kuhn

ISBN: 978-1-60486-111-2
$26.95   352 pages

The defeat in World War I and the subsequent end of the Kaiserreich threw Germany into turmoil. While the Social Democrats grabbed power, radicals across the country rallied to establish a socialist society under the slogan "All Power to the Councils!" The Spartacus League staged an uprising in Berlin, council republics were proclaimed in Bremen and Bavaria, and workers' revolts shook numerous German towns. The rebellions were crushed by the Social Democratic government with the help of right-wing militias like the notorious Free Corps. This paved the way to a dysfunctional Weimar Republic that witnessed the rise of the National Socialist movement.

The documentary history presented here collects manifestos, speeches, articles, and letters from the German Revolution, introduced and annotated by the editor. Many documents, like the anarchist Erich Mühsam's comprehensive account of the Bavarian Council Republic, are made available in English for the first time. The volume also includes appendixes portraying the Red Ruhr Army that repelled the reactionary Kapp Putsch in 1920, and the communist bandits that roamed Eastern Germany until 1921. *All Power to the Councils!* provides a dynamic and vivid picture of a time with long-lasting effects for world history. A time that was both encouraging and tragic.

"The councils of the early 20th century, as they are presented in this volume, were autonomous organs of the working class beyond the traditional parties and unions. They had stepped out of the hidden world of small political groups and represented a mass movement fighting for an all-encompassing council system."
—Teo Panther, editor of *Alle Macht den Räten: Novemberrevolution 1918*

"The German Revolution of 1918-1919 and the following years mark an exceptional period in German history. This collection brings the radical aspirations of the time alive and contains many important lessons for contemporary scholars and activists alike."
—Markus Bauer, Free Workers' Union, FAU-IAA

Sober Living for the Revolution: Hardcore Punk, Straight Edge and Radical Politics

Edited by Gabriel Kuhn

ISBN: 978-1-60486-051-1
$22.95   304 pages

Straight edge has persisted as a drug-free, hardcore punk subculture for 25 years. Its political legacy, however, remains ambiguous—often associated with self-righteous macho posturing and conservative puritanism. While certain elements of straight edge culture feed into such perception, the movement's political history is far more complex. Since straight edge's origins in Washington, D.C. in the early 1980s, it has been linked to radical thought and action by countless individuals, bands, and entire scenes worldwide. *Sober Living for the Revolution* traces this history.

It includes contributions—in the form of in-depth interviews, essays, and manifestos—by numerous artists and activists connected to straight edge, from Ian MacKaye (Minor Threat/Fugazi) and Mark Andersen (*Dance of Days*/Positive Force DC) to Dennis Lyxzén (Refused/The (International) Noise Conspiracy) and Andy Hurley (Racetraitor/Fall Out Boy), from bands such as ManLiftingBanner and Point of No Return to feminist and queer initiatives, from radical collectives like CrimethInc. and Alpine Anarchist Productions to the Emancypunx project and many others dedicated as much to sober living as to the fight for a better world.

"Perhaps the greatest reason I am still committed to sXe is an unfailing belief that sXe is more than music, that it can be a force of change. I believe in the power of sXe as a bridge to social change, as an opportunity to create a more just and sustainable world."
—Ross Haenfler, Professor of Sociology at the University of Mississippi, author of *Straight Edge: Clean-Living Youth, Hardcore Punk, And Social Change*

"An 'ecstatic sobriety' which combats the dreariness of one and the bleariness of the other—false pleasure and false discretion alike—is analogous to the anarchism that confronts both the false freedom offered by capitalism and the false community offered by communism."
—CrimethInc. Ex-Workers' Collective

Soccer vs. the State: Tackling Football and Radical Politics

Gabriel Kuhn

ISBN: 978-1-60486-053-5
$20.00   264 pages

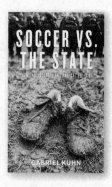

Soccer has turned into a multi-billion
dollar industry. Professionalism and
commercialization dominate its global image.
Yet the game retains a rebellious side, maybe
more so than any other sport co-opted by
money makers and corrupt politicians. From its roots in working-class
England to political protests by players and fans, and a current radical
soccer underground, the notion of football as the "people's game" has
been kept alive by numerous individuals, teams, and communities.
This book not only traces this history, but also reflects on common
criticisms: soccer ferments nationalism, serves right-wing powers,
fosters competitiveness. Acknowledging these concerns, alternative
perspectives on the game are explored, down to practical examples of
egalitarian DIY soccer!

Soccer vs. the State serves both as an orientation for the politically
conscious football supporter and as an inspiration for those who try to
pursue the love of the game away from television sets and big stadiums,
bringing it to back alleys and muddy pastures.

*"There is no sport that reflects the place where sports and politics collide
quite like soccer. Athlete-activist Gabriel Kuhn has captured that by going
to a place where other sports writers fear to tread. Here is the book that will
tell you how soccer explains the world while offering means to improve it."*
—Dave Zirin, author *Bad Sports: How Owners are Ruining the Games We
Love*

*"I was greatly encouraged by this work. It provided me with alternative
ways to play, enjoy, and talk about football, leaving behind nationalism
and the exclusiveness of elite athletes. When we applied the clues and tips
included here to the anti-G8 football matches in Japan in 2008, we were
able to communicate, interact, and connect with many people, regardless
of nationality, race, and religion. I recommend this book to all who seriously
hope for an alternative space in sports. Unite the world through football,
and reclaim sports!"*
—Minobu, Rage Football Collective (RFC), Japan